IN SEARCH
OF TRUTH
& LOVE

IN SEARCH
OF TRUTH
& LOVE

Jae R. Ballif

Bookcraft
Salt Lake City, Utah

Library of Congress Catalog Card Number: 86-71659

ISBN 0-88494-607-X

First Printing, 1986

Printed in the United States of America

Contents

            Given Organizations

       9 ‖ The Family   105

      10 ‖ The Church of Jesus Christ of
            Latter-day Saints   118

         ‖ Afterword   127

         ‖ Appendix: The Organizations and
            Ordinances of the Church   129

         ‖ Index   145

Preface

It is useful, I believe, for all of us to pause from time to time and evaluate where we are and where we are going. It is even more useful if the evaluation is made while we still have a good way to go. These few pages synthesize what I believe at this point in my life to be the most important things I have come to know.

Earlier in my life I found a very large number of ideas, principles, and programs of almost consuming importance. I still find an increasing number of subjects that I know little about that are of intense interest. However, I find fewer and fewer ideas and principles to be of fundamental value.

In some ways life is extraordinarily simple. At least, the governing principles are simple. At the same time, the applications and details are so numerous and complicated that we are often overwhelmed. What is known of the central principles that give meaning and purpose to all of life is accessible to everyone.

I am stunned by the beauty and organization of nature. I am awed by the principles that have been discovered that accurately describe and predict occurrences in nature. I am even more impressed with the accomplishments and the nobility of men and women who learn and practice the few fundamental principles that govern progress in perfecting the soul, direct appropriate relationships between people, and set forth the ultimate possibility for us all.

I am already justified in my effort to evaluate, because I now have a more clear understanding of life and its purpose.

If my views encourage others to evaluate their lives

and then pursue truth more effectively so that they come to recognize the nobility and the capability of men and women participating in the mortal phase of a divine plan, it will be an added source of happiness.

Acknowledgments

Many people have helped me in the preparation of this manuscript, and I acknowledge with deep gratitude their contributions. I cannot list every name, for that list would of necessity include all the significant people of my life, but I do not forget them.

This material has been shaped throughout the years by the stimulating exchange of ideas I have enjoyed with my colleagues at Brigham Young University and my associates in Church assignments. Many of them have studied at least part of this manuscript and made significant contributions to its contents.

Some of my most meaningful study of the gospel came while presiding over the mission in New England. There, enlightened by the Spirit of the Lord, and challenged by the humility and devotion of the missionaries who served with me, I came to feel a great desire to write this book.

With love I gratefully acknowledge the encouragement of my dear wife, Carma, and our seven wonderful children and their companions. We have discussed these matters together on many occasions and I have learned from their comments, from their questions, and from their lives.

Also with love I acknowledge my beloved parents, who taught me gospel principles and by example awakened in me the great quest for harmony in all truth.

I am very grateful to my sister, Moana Bennett, for hours of stimulating discussion and for her superb editorial assistance.

I express appreciation for the able help of my secretary, Doris Astin, in the preparation of the text.

I am also indebted to the editors at Bookcraft for their careful reading and thoughtful editing of the manuscript.

Finally, I humbly acknowledge the giver of all truth for His profound influence.

Part One

On
Considering
Truth

Chapter One

The Gospel of Jesus Christ Includes All True Principles

For centuries the word *gospel* has been used in English translations of the Bible for the Hebrew word meaning "glad tidings" and the Greek word meaning "good news," and has been scripturally defined basically as news of the redeeming sacrifice of the Savior Jesus Christ. This is the central message of the Restoration. In bringing back to the world the fulness of the gospel, the Prophet Joseph Smith gave to the world a new testimony of this great hope-filled truth and extended mankind's understanding of the teachings of Jesus Christ.

One of the most meaningful concepts I have come to understand is that the gospel of Jesus Christ includes all true principles: those of deepest significance, such as the truth of the Resurrection, and all of the fascinating principles by which the world was created.

As a physicist I welcome the freedom that this understanding gives to me. I do not have to choose between "godless science" and "unscientific religion." My full energies can be spent in striving to learn that which I do not know and in constantly sharpening my ability to determine what is true and what is not true.

Truth Exists and Governs

There are true principles that account for and govern all things as they were, as they are, and as they are to be. These principles exist independently of the human mind.

The gospel of Jesus Christ is a name which applies to this entire set of true principles.

Some true principles are more important for us to understand now than others. They constitute the central message of God's revelations to mankind. They define the relationship of men and women to God, outline the redeeming sacrifice of Jesus Christ, and establish the principles that govern the perfecting of the soul. Often, in the scriptures, the word *gospel* has been used to identify only these essential principles. These are the principles of highest priority.

Through His prophets God has revealed again what mankind has understood before: true principles exist. The great significance of this position, to me, is that beginning with the belief that there are true principles, mankind may proceed with the faith that it is possible to learn what is true. Knowing that true principles exist compels me to seek them. As men and women engage in the search for these eternal, true principles, they succeed in small but identifiable steps. Every success brings greater validity to the search and greater understanding to us, individually.

It seems to me that the alternative assumption—that there are no true principles—constrains mankind to a suffocating life of doubt, uncertainty, superstition, and despair. Such negativism prompts people to justify continued cataloguing of mankind's failures. However, no matter how long lists become, they will not prove that true principles do not exist. They will prove only that by our assuming true principles do not exist and failing to make the search, they cannot be found.

Another position suggests that all true principles are relative. This is a very old argument. It is a position like quicksand, without stability and without substance. It is a position taken when we tend to confuse the existence of true principles with the possession of true principles. In our awareness of the difficulties we have encountered in our own efforts to learn what is true, we often question or deny the very existence of true principles. Then our motivation to continue the difficult pursuit of true principles decreases. We begin to accept the wrong but more comfortable position that all statements of belief are equally true. I believe the result of this position is, finally, little different from the assumption that there are no true principles.

In the restoration of the wholeness of the gospel, God has reaffirmed this fundamental truth: true principles are independent of our belief, our preference, our understanding, or our cultural environment. This understanding propels us into a dynamic, positive, lifelong search that demands of us continued enlargement of our intellects and of our souls. Eliminating from our thinking the idea that true principles are established by our preference, by our perception, or by majority vote sharpens our focus.

We can influence many things, including whether we ever come to know true principles. However, we cannot change the fact that true principles exist. For instance, our understanding or acceptance of the principle of gravitational interaction does not change the fact that the forces of gravity hold moons in their orbits around planets and determine the motion of falling objects.

Another concept of great importance is that this set of true principles, which exists, governs all things. Some of this set of principles explain and govern the physical universe and some explain and govern the inhabitants of the universe. True principles govern the changes that occur in the history of a star and true principles govern the changes that occur in the development of a man or a woman. All things as they once were, as they are at this time, and as they will come to be are subject to and governed by these principles.

These principles do not have independent intelligence and agency. There are bounds and conditions associated with them. God has power to bring about His purposes because He understands these principles and how to use them.

The existence of such principles does not mean that we are unable to alter the course of our lives. It does not mean there is always a simple explanation of relationship between causes and effects in the events of life. Nor does it mean that we are insignificant in the outcome of an event. It does mean that neither nature nor God is chaotic or capricious.

It is important to realize that in one sense it is the full set of true principles which is the gospel of Jesus Christ. The gospel of Jesus Christ is also known as the word of God. God speaks only that which is true. He makes true principles available to us through His word. He often makes these true principles available to us only when we carefully observe and diligently study. We learn precept upon precept, but we will not understand the full majesty of the gospel nor the complete glad tidings of Jesus Christ until we come to an understanding of all true principles. Sometimes, in the course of diligent study and honest questioning, God opens our understanding beyond what we had conceived.

I have come to realize that true principles and facts are not synonymous. There are many statements which accurately describe a condition or situation; however, this information is not necessarily a principle. Nevertheless, the condition or situation did result from the effects of conforming to or violating true principles, whether the principles were known or hidden. It is important to differentiate between observations, facts, and principles.

True Principles Are Independent of Time

There never was a time when true principles did not exist.

There never will be a time when true principles will not exist.

God has given us the understanding that true principles were not invented nor decreed. They always have existed with Him. They are eternal. For example, there never was a time when gravitational forces did not exist. The ultimate true principles continue the same yesterday, today, and forever. Worlds and civilizations come into being, change, and may even be destroyed, but throughout all time the ultimate true principles do not change. This, I believe, is extremely significant because it makes clear that even though much of what we experience involves change, there are principles that do not change, and it makes clear that by continuing the search we can understand these governing principles.

I am aware that "special" phenomena do occur and are observed. Changes in conditions often change what we observe. I am also aware that we are immersed in complex situations, relationships, and organizations in which unique applications make it extremely difficult to understand the simplicity, beauty, and power of the more fundamental principles. Even so, as we continue to probe we learn more and more about the underlying principles that do account for and govern all things. Time after time scientists have found that earlier statements based on careful observations of what appeared to be absolute have needed revision.

As our tools for more precise observation and measurements have improved and as our capacity to observe and to understand has enlarged, our first descriptions have been recognized as approximate statements, and a more accurate articulation has become possible.

As an illustration, direct observations of objects about us give us the impression that matter is solid and continuous. Under a microscope it becomes apparent that matter is not solid but is made up of many invisible particles in various states of motion called molecules. Tiny objects suspended in a liquid or a gas are observed to be jostled about by molecules colliding with them. More careful observations make it clear that molecules themselves are combinations of even smaller particles called atoms. Even atoms are found to be made up of matter particles called electrons, protons, and neutrons. In a more accurate experiment performed with more sophisticated equipment, beams of high-energy, electrically charged particles were passed through a very thin gold foil. In this experiment, it was learned that even atoms are mostly empty. The atom consists of a surprisingly small electrically charged particle called the nucleus and oppositely charged electrons that surround the nucleus at relatively large distances. Still more sophisticated experiments have taught us that even the particles making up the atom are not smooth continuous objects. It is now clear that they also have structure. Furthermore, they somehow behave as both particles and space-filling waves.

It is also my observation that as I have studied and attempted to practice the rules of love taught by Christ, my capacity to love has enlarged and at the same time the principles that govern human relationships have become more clear to me.

The principles that govern changes of all kinds remain unchanged. They are independent of all time. But it is perfectly clear that our perception of some things does change.

Truth Is Consistent

All true principles are part of one great, consistent, indivisible framework of truth.

True principles cannot conflict.

True principles are often composites.

All True Principles Are Part of One Framework of Truth

Contemplation of the revelation that all true principles belong to the gospel of Jesus Christ has led me to understand that there are relatively few governing principles but nearly endless applications. We are subject to a vast number of special cases and must struggle to see beyond the immediate circumstances to the more fundamental universal true principles.

Such principles cannot conflict. They are all parts of one integrated framework. When apparent conflicts arise, they are due to our limited understanding, or they occur because we now believe some things that are untrue. With this view, times of apparent conflict become times of great expectation and optimism because by believing that a resolution of the discrepancy exists, we who search are on the threshold of greater enlightenment.

Our search for true principles is often complicated by limitations we inaccurately perceive or inappropriately conceive. The boundary of proper concern is the boundary between truth and error. If we set up other boundaries they often become oppressive walls that confine and limit us, and, more significant, they prevent us from ever finding the harmony of true principles.

For me, one of the inappropriate and very unfortunate walls that has been built is along the boundary between that which is called ''religious'' and that which is called ''secular.'' The word of God says to me that if something is true, it is religious. It is part of that eternal truth known and taught by God. True science is part of true religion. Ultimately the laws that govern the universe are part of the framework of the true principles known and used by God. His is a perfect science because He knows the ultimate laws which govern. Because we do not yet fully understand, we establish false boundaries between segments of approximations to true governing principles.

True Principles Cannot Conflict

When the Creation is finally understood, it will be clear that there is a set of eternal laws that govern the universe and that God, understanding these laws, accomplished the Creation by working within the bounds and conditions of these laws. The gospel of Jesus Christ takes on beautiful, new dimensions for me with the realization that it includes all true principles, and that these principles are harmonious. I find it exciting that the principles that govern the strong interaction between the particles in the nucleus of an atom and the principles that govern relationships between people are all part of the gospel and cannot conflict with each other or with any other true principle.

The light of the gospel makes it clear that we cannot accept either a "godless science" or an "unscientific religion." I believe that understanding the harmony of true principles lets us pursue our continuing search for wisdom from a much stronger position. I reject the view that life on earth is the result of chance, devoid of divine influence. I also reject the view that the Creator formed the earth and man out of nothing, in conflict with the observable, describable laws of nature.

The gospel of Jesus Christ brings forth a grander view. Under the direction of God, Jesus Christ organized the world in harmony with eternal laws. The earth was prepared for a specific purpose. The organization took place in planned phases, and when the earth was fully prepared Adam became the first spirit child of God to live on earth. We, who have followed Adam here, are in the image of God and have the capacity to become as He is. We are here to learn to choose and to practice true principles in acts of love. We are here to develop the attributes of Jesus Christ.

There are many great and important things yet to be revealed. God, referring to His creations, has promised that "all their glories, laws, and set times shall be revealed."

When God set man and woman upon the mortal experience, He commanded them to subdue the earth. He knew that to subdue the earth they must come to understand and to know the laws that govern it. It would violate a true principle (that which we struggle to understand, we come to know) if He were to detail the laws of His creation for this world. However, He does give us, His children, courage to continue to search, reassuring us that, indeed, such knowledge can be found, for it does exist, and that as it is learned the apparent conflicts will be resolved. He offers to us the encouragement that such an ongoing search is of value. He has revealed to us that uncovering and then mastering all true principles is the purpose of creation. Of course no one is able to discover all true principles in this life, but we can each begin to learn all things, building our understanding concept upon concept.

As one who has studied the body of knowledge we call physics (a study of the fundamental principles that govern phenomena in the physical world), I am convinced that if we search diligently we will slowly but surely come to know the laws which govern the universe. I am convinced that as we come to know these laws, inconsistencies and apparent conflicts will be fully resolved.

As one who loves the word of God, I am thoughtfully aware that tangled relationships of men and women, and of nations, can also yield to a wholehearted application of the eternal principle of love. I am convinced that we are capable of coming to know and of putting into practice those universal true principles concerning mankind that will overcome many of the conditions which bring conflict and misery.

All that I have learned declares to me that the real challenge and task before us is to separate true principles from error and then to apply each principle in loving service.

True Principles Are Often Composites

Another profoundly significant truth is that true principles are often a composite of more than one important part. A superficial or simplistic view leads to a world full of apparent paradoxes. A more accurate view allows for the innate multiplicity that exists in the nature of all things and makes clear the harmony that characterizes all that is true.

There are two especially important dimensions of this significant concept, the composite nature of things. Most of us are acquainted with this idea from simple illustrations suggesting choices between right and wrong or good and evil. These illustrations are frequently given to make clear the fact that we do have the right, the responsibility, and the power of choice.

A second aspect of the idea that is less often understood is that the very nature of things includes a multiplicity in one. This composite nature is well known to those who study matter and radiation. Such studies show that matter and radiation have both a wave and a particle nature. Experiments can be designed to illustrate the lumpiness or particle nature of things. Other experiments can be designed to show that there is a space-filling wave aspect to their nature.

We describe matter and radiation by the properties we observe when they interact with other matter and radiation. In different circumstances different properties are observed. A true set of principles must account for all properties.

As I have listened to the problems people struggle with and examined some I struggle with as well, over and over I am reminded of the composite nature of all things. For example, we experience both sorrow and joy when we develop charitable love for others. We are both completely dependent upon God for everything of value and completely responsible to determine the success of our lives. We are at the same time just a little lower than the angels and also capable of being evil, sensual, and devilish.

The attributes we observe in ourselves and others are made known as we interact with others. In different circumstances, different attributes are observed. True principles must account for all these attributes.

There is no lack of harmony in this multiplicity. However, the harmony cannot be observed until we understand the more accurate set of true principles that set forth the nature of things. If we understand the composite nature of things we can work past the apparent contradictions. In so doing, we will find an internal peace and joy even as we struggle with the complexities of life. If we do not understand the composite nature of many things, we can distort partial truth until it prevents progress or until we become too discouraged to continue and thus fail in the very purpose of life.

Truth Can Be Learned

It is possible to learn true principles not known before.

It is possible to separate true principles from error.

There are principles that, when followed, prepare us for a discerning spirit that helps us identify truth.

Truth is acquired in successive approximations. The process, if continued, is self-correcting so that we are led to more and more fundamental principles.

Truth acquired but not properly used can be lost.

I find that it is profoundly important to know not only that true principles exist but also that it is possible to learn what they are, how to understand them, and how to use them. I believe it is possible to sort out that which is true from that which is in error. The specific process that leads to truth will be discussed in detail in a later chapter. The process requires the appropriate application of several true principles. Searching souls who proceed in harmony with these principles have access to a discerning spirit that allows them to identify and to understand that which is true.

I do not believe that an understanding of true principles is easily acquired. To come to a complete understanding of all true principles is not possible in mortality. Therefore, the pursuit of a knowledge of true principles becomes a continuing process here and extends into post-mortal eternity. Fortunately, the process allows continuous self-correction. As the unknown becomes known, ignorance is replaced by knowledge and superstition loses its restricting influence on men and women. We can observe inconsistencies which lead us to recognize errors. Identifying errors is the first step toward eliminating them. If individuals and groups allow the self-correcting aspects of their search process to end, they deprive themselves of the exhilaration, joy, and additional opportunities that come with each new glimpse of that which is true. Self-interests and ignorance exaggerate errors. When this happens, the result is usually that true principles are distorted and eventually lost. When truth is lost, individuals lose their strength and cultures disintegrate.

As we pursue the process that leads to true principles, our minds are enlightened. The true principles revealed illuminate the darkness of both misunderstanding and error. For me this great process of coming to know that which is true is like coming from the darkness into the beautiful light of day. Misunderstandings, superstition, and the constraints of ignorance give way to freedom, knowledge, and opportunity to make still further progress. It is most appropriate to associate that which is true with light.

True principles are not communicated through words alone. We often come to a more complete understanding of a principle when both our minds and our senses are enlightened through an experience. These extensions of our understanding come bursting upon us as we see, feel, and hear, and as we interact with people, nature, events, and artistic expressions of great insight. Profound experiences open us to sensitivities, relationships, and significant implications which otherwise we might miss.

Experiences of importance in enlarging our understanding of true principles come to us in many ways. Sometimes it is an individual contemplation of a sequence of personal observations; sometimes it is in interacting with others; sometimes it is a series of events that gives us enlarged vision.

Many times it is in enjoying the magnificence and beauty of nature, from the vastness of the heavens to the intricacy of a cell, that we come to a greater awareness of the sense of harmony in the laws that govern natural creation even before we understand them.

Experiences with great art (including theatre, literature, painting, sculpture, music, and dance) may refine our understanding and may bring us to a greater understanding of true principles. Great art enables us to transcend our current existence. It gives us insight into the human experience from many perspectives. It directs our attention to the wonder of the eternal uniqueness of each individual soul. Sometimes the human molding of experience into an artistic expression brings to us glimpses of the majesty and the mystery of life and nature in such a way as to give us a richer and fuller understanding of some true principles. Such artistic expressions strengthen and lift the soul and give vision, which renews us and extends our reach for understanding of governing principles.

As in all approaches to true principles, the individual must evaluate these experiences for their essential harmony. It is only through this evaluation that one can discover whether these experiences are to be helpful in encouraging this eternal quest. We must struggle to discipline our minds and our senses to be receptive. The process that leads to understanding these principles applies to the full range of experiences, including those that allow our senses to contribute to our understanding. The full light of truth envelops our whole being.

Chapter Two

‖ Corollaries Exist That Are
‖ Derived from Truth

I believe the existence of this framework of true principles carries with it certain corollaries.

There Are Eternal Values

‖ Values independent of time or culture exist
‖ because true principles exist.

Eternal values are associated with true principles and are not the result of cultural evolution. For example, I believe ideals such as integrity, morality, wisdom, and love for others have been, are, and forever will be true values. They exist because true principles exist. Stealing another's name, possessions, or virtue can never be consistent with eternal values even if a society accepts such behavior. Social or majority preference is not enough to justify a value system. Agreement or consensus among people is not sufficient to determine true values. Enduring values are those that are consistent with eternal true principles. Societies that do not have, or that have had and lost, these eternal values become decadent and chaotic. When integrity, wisdom, and love give way to selfishness and ignorance, people are engulfed in a darkness that is far more inhibiting than the natural phenomenon of nightfall.

There Are Eternal Laws

True principles frequently constitute eternal laws, with their associated bounds and conditions.

Both God and man are bound by eternal laws.

Knowing and choosing to live in harmony with eternal laws brings both power and freedom.

I believe that some true principles are eternal, governing laws. These laws prescribe what is possible and how we must proceed in order to accomplish what is possible.

Civil laws are not necessarily consistent with eternal laws. When civil law approximates eternal law the people are greatly blessed.

I have come to appreciate that there are bounds and conditions associated with eternal law. I see that the results of an event are related to the special conditions that exist. Both God and man are bound by these conditions. God is not capricious. He lives by principle. He is bound by true principles just as we are. When we learn and live by eternal law we are inevitably blessed; and, more important, we become more like God, who always lives by law. When we violate the conditions of eternal law we are subject to the inevitable consequences of transgressing true principles.

I believe knowing and choosing to live in harmony with the bounds and conditions of eternal law brings both power and freedom. The understanding of greater law allows us to influence conditions in ways consistent with true principles and to bring about desired results. In this sense the understanding of true principles is power. The understanding of eternal law and its associated bounds and conditions makes it possible to choose to live in harmony with true principles, a choice that brings freedom: freedom from the inevitable consequence of violating true principles, and freedom to use the understanding acquired to provide opportunity for self and others. I do not see true principles as restricting or as stifling to the human experience. Rather, it seems to me, knowing true principles and choosing to use them makes possible a wide range of opportunities not otherwise possible. Consider these illustrations from the scientific discoveries of man.

Not long ago the illness poliomyelitis brought great fear among us because its crippling effects are so debilitating. Understanding the bounds and conditions of the illness and the physiological laws that apply has made it possible for us to control the environment in a limited way. This knowledge gives power. We are now able to be free from the effects of the disease. The restrictions of the disease came about not only from the physical disabilities suffered by those who contracted it but also from the fear of contracting the disease, which at one time was rampant.

An astronaut participating in a flight to the moon is bound by the laws that govern such motion. If he or those able to control his craft do not slow his speed in the right way as he approaches the earth's atmosphere, he will not arrive at the recovery point on the earth's surface as planned. Instead, he may well spiral into the corona of the sun and suffer the consequences of that inhospitable environment. All his good intentions and pleading will not give him the power and freedom to go to the moon and return to his loved ones safely. This power and freedom is gained only by the use of knowledge and behavior that is in harmony with the bounds and conditions of the eternal laws which govern such motion.

There Are Commandments

|| Commandments are brief statements of direction
|| given by God that are consistent with eternal laws.

Our limited understanding and our agency require that some true principles be made accessible to us immediately. Such limited but immediately accessible truth is given to guide us away from making decisions that result in violation of eternal principles. I see commandments as insight given to us by a loving Eternal Father to provide us protection while we learn. Commandments are consistent with, but different in scope from, eternal laws.

I do not believe commandments are imposed. Rather, they are given for our consideration and by way of instruction. We are invited to act on them, to use them, and to test them. In all cases the individual is responsible to choose. This agency, responsibility, and right of choice between eternal law and alternatives is itself an eternal principle. Commandments are provided to make it possible for us to choose even when our knowledge is yet limited by our ignorance. In this way commandments are brief statements of profound, eternal, true principles.

For example, "Thou shalt love thy neighbor as thyself" is a commandment. It takes time to understand the greater principle of true love or charity. It takes even longer to apply it appropriately. To guide us, to suggest some of the implications of the fuller law, and to protect us while we learn, the commandment expresses in a terse statement what we should do and how we should evaluate what we do.

Evil Exists Because Truth Exists

Another important explanation that comes from our knowledge about the nature of true principles concerns the existence of evil.

|| Evil is a result of sin: sin is the conscious violation of a true principle.

When we come to an understanding of a true principle we are immediately faced with a new responsibility. We are then capable of consciously choosing between true principles and error. If we choose to conform to true principles, we progress and bring good into the world. If we choose error, we sin and are responsible for increasing evil in the world.

Evil exists not because God has created an imperfect world but because we choose to do evil. The great struggle between good and evil goes on as we make choices and thereby subject ourselves either to those who encourage us to do good or to those who desire that we join them in bringing evil into the world.

Suffering Exists Because Eternal Law Exists

One of the most important explanations that comes from our knowledge about the nature of true principles concerns the nature of suffering. We all suffer from time to time. Suffering envelops us and makes us feel very much alone. Because it seems so inconsistent with our expectations and so unnecessary, suffering also causes us to re-evaluate our beliefs. Therefore, it is very important to understand the experience of suffering. There are at least three definitions that are useful:

> *Sorrow* is experienced when:
> — We are separated from those we love.
> — We observe innocent suffering.
>
> *Misery* is experienced when we violate eternal law.
>
> *Pain* is experienced in mortality because:
> — Here we are subject to the physical laws that make mortality a finite interval.
> — Others commit evil acts.

Many are aware that there is suffering in the world. To many, the existence of suffering denies the existence of God. Some people say, "If there is a loving God, why does He allow suffering?" This often leads to agnosticism or even atheism. An assumption that God created everything out of nothing means that He also must have created evil and suffering. This brings us to a dilemma in many ways intolerable. I believe such a notion tempts us to believe that God either does not exist or that He is capricious and irresponsible. It is my conviction that neither condition is true. We who have come into mortality made the choice to do so knowing that we would be subject to mortal law. Still, we chose to come. In this environment we are exposed to at least three kinds of suffering.

Sorrow Is One Kind of Suffering

As we develop the capacity to love one another, and then are separated from those we love, we sorrow. The more godly our life, the more susceptible we are to this sorrow, and the more severe the sorrow experienced. We can be separated by distance, physical death, or sin. If the separation is temporary, we experience great joy when we are reunited. In this age to be separated by distance has become a relatively minor problem. Communication is abundantly available and transportation which conquers distance quickly gives individuals access to one another. These facts soften the sorrow of separation by distance.

In the death of someone we love, we experience a deeper sorrow. We are aware that the separation will last for an extended interval. We also know there is only rarely any communication with the one who has died. Because we love the absent ones, we are very sorrowful.

When those we love choose error and separate themselves from us and from God, there is the possibility of an eternal separation that could last even beyond death. This makes the sorrow even more severe and long-lasting. A conscious choice of error is sin, and it brings about the most difficult and long-lasting separations.

Jesus Christ, who experiences great joy when we progress, also sometimes suffers intensely from sorrow. His suffering is for the sins of all of us, sins that separate us from Him unless they are overcome. Though we may know this kind of sorrow, at this time we cannot know either the extent or the intensity of the sorrow Jesus Christ experiences.

We cannot be free from sorrow and succeed in the purpose of life. Our task is to learn to love, and the more deeply we love the more vulnerable we are to sorrow. The sorrow we experience when those whom we love commit sin is for both the transgressors, who bring evil into the world, and for the innocent, who are caused to suffer because of the effect of sin. The innocent who suffer will eventually be given compensating opportunity, but for an interval they are deprived because others have abused the right to choose.

Misery Is a Kind of Suffering

Misery is a suffering we bring on ourselves. We do not need to have this kind of suffering. Misery is experienced by those of us who know truth and choose error. Whatever temporary pleasure is derived from the choice, sin is ultimately followed by misery. When we do not meet the bounds and conditions of law, we suffer the consequences and we know misery. There is no peace except in repentance for those of us who violate law. Sin leads to misery for the sinner and to sorrow for those who love the one who sins.

The ultimate misery brought about by sin is experienced now by Lucifer, whom we know as Satan. God, our Eternal Father, knows him as His son. Satan has brought upon himself an eternal separation and a condition of continual suffering. This condition is hell. It is the inevitable consequence of being separated from God and those we love by conscious choices that are in violation of true principles. There will be a time when all will be aware of the consequences of their own sins. This awareness will constitute hell for those who have not overcome their errors.

Pain Is Also a Kind of Suffering

There is yet another kind of suffering that we are subject to in our mortal state. This world and the people in it are subject to illness, disease, and calamity. As we come to understand eternal laws, we can partially protect ourselves from pain. For example, by better diets we can reduce illness and delay death. God has counseled us that we will be healthier if we refrain from smoking and from drinking alcoholic beverages and if we will include in our diets fruits, vegetables, grains, and occasionally meat. Experience justifies our efforts to follow His counsel. Nevertheless, we are still subject to illness and death because our mortal condition must end in death.

Sometimes God intercedes. He knows the greater law and can influence what happens by His appropriate application of true principles. However, He does not always intercede. Ill health is not an evidence that God has judged us as being unrighteous. If, in God's greater perspective, it is not appropriate to alter the conditions, then the uninfluenced effect of the law governs. Thus we experience illness and suffer pain. If this were not so, choice would be taken from us, and choice, or agency, is itself an eternal principle. If the righteous were always healed, the evidence would impel everyone to respond to the Lord's commandments. In that case His purpose—to give us an environment in which we would grow by learning to discern truth from error and choosing to live in harmony with it—would be thwarted.

Innocent Suffering Is Another Form of Pain

Some suffer from another's choice. Since God allows us to have choice in mortality, it is possible for some people to abuse others. We are all well aware of the terrible suffering that the choices of some impose on others. In mortality people can cause physical and emotional pain that seems almost beyond our ability to bear. God sorrows as He observes both violations of eternal law and the pain that it causes. Nevertheless, He is committed to agency for all in order that each might choose to be either just or unjust. Only occasionally does God intrude into the affairs of men and women. He weeps for those who suffer pain at the hands of others. He weeps for those who perpetrate evil acts. In one sense, He suffers even more for the latter group because He knows they are separating themselves from Him. Those who endure pain and succeed in accomplishing the purpose of mortal life will be with Him again. They will have an internal peace now and eternal opportunity in the life hereafter even though they have suffered innocently.

We entered mortality informed that we would struggle during our existence here. We chose to participate in this life. We knew that mortal laws would cause suffering for both the just and the unjust. I believe that even before mortality we caught a glimpse of the vision of eternal progression, which excited our souls for the adventure ahead. We knew that any injustice experienced in mortality would be compensated for at a later time.

We can influence the amount of pain suffered in this life by learning all that we can and by using that knowledge wisely; and by treating other people as God has treated us. Our efforts will not always protect us from pain. Our challenge remains to reach beyond the pain to an understanding of the purpose of life and to discipline our souls toward that ongoing search for all true principles in spite of the acts of others and the conditions of mortality. The balm of Gilead, or solace offered by God, is the peace which passeth understanding and which He will send to those who seek Him. It will comfort us and give us vision, and it will keep alive hope sufficient to continue.

Joy Exists Because Truth Exists

Still another important explanation that follows from our understanding of the nature of truth concerns the source of joy.

|| Joy is experienced when we and those we love
|| understand and choose to live in harmony with
|| true principles.

It seems to me that in all lands and at all times the activities
people choose are accurate expressions of their search for
happiness. People pursue what they value with the expectation that by acquiring those things they will be more
happy. Happiness is related to our state of well-being and
satisfaction. Therefore, what we value and strive for does
determine our state of happiness.

We should strive to find happiness. Whether we
actually find it depends on what we come to value and how
we pursue the search. We are capable of pursuing values
that will bring happiness even though we cannot control
everything in our lives. Frequently poverty, calamity, and
frustration are due to natural disasters or to the decisions
of others. Nevertheless, we can attain greater and greater
happiness by assuming the responsibility for our reactions
to such events and by initiating the actions which lead us
toward the attainment of eternal values.

It is important to keep in mind the difference between happiness of short duration, which is pleasure, and
happiness that endures through time, which is joy. Many
things give pleasure but have no real value in building joy
into one's life. The important evaluation of a pursuit is
whether selfish aggrandizement dominates it. If it is gratification of a momentary nature, then one needs to be concerned whether it be sought in terms of wealth, power,
leisure activities, or satisfaction of bodily appetites. Those
who are selfish are seldom content with what they have
acquired. Those who value truth and the well-being of
others find happiness that persists. They achieve peace
and find joy in spite of adversity. They experience an enduring satisfaction that is unknown to the selfish. Joy and
peace are experienced as we learn true principles, choose
to live in harmony with them, and use them in providing

opportunities for others that will help them experience enduring happiness also.

Joy and sorrow are inseparable companions. Both are experienced as a result of our love for others. The more true principles we know and follow, the more capable we are of loving others. The more we love others, the more susceptible we are to both joy and sorrow. When those we love accept true principles and bring their lives into harmony with them, we feel joy. Their relationship with us and with God is closer. We become more unified as we understand and accept eternal principles.

The realization that true principles exist and are accessible to those who search, and that following these principles is accompanied by peace and freedom, brings exuberance, eager expectation, and quiet strength to life. The anticipation of greater joy by those who devote their lives to learning the principles and loving others is always rewarded.

Chapter Three

The Process by Which True Principles Are Discovered

One of the most crucial revelations which God has given to man, in my judgment, is the revelation which introduces us to the process by which we can discover that which is truth. It is my experience that there is only one process for the discovering of truth, and that this process functions with equal validity in all areas of study. However, it is also my observation that there is a significant difference in some of the activities in which we participate as we engage this universal process, and this sometimes leads to confusion as to the universality of the process and the principles involved.

In this chapter I will outline the principles of the process as I have come to recognize them while I have searched for that which is true in my study of physics and in my study of the scriptures. I believe the process works equally well in all searches for true concepts. One of the most intriguing aspects of such recognition, for me, has been the unfolding realization that these are the same principles which also govern the perfecting of one's talents and the perfecting of one's own soul.

It is important, I believe, to examine first the process as it applies to discerning true concepts and true principles. Understanding each true concept is a prerequisite to any progress in continuing the search for an understanding of all things. It is also a prerequisite for living according to true principles. Jesus Christ said we learn precept upon precept. Mankind's experience with learning verifies this principle. In science today we stand, as Sir Isaac Newton, the physicist, said, on the shoulders of the giants who have preceded us. Clearly the mastery of all things is a goal reached by increments.

It also seems plain to me that every bit of light and knowledge which we come to understand brings with it the responsibility of making it available to others. Madame Curie, the great Polish-French scientist, isolated radium. It was proposed that she and her husband patent the technique and thus reap great monetary return. She replied that her knowledge was to be shared with all mankind. When the heavens opened in response to the modern Prophet Joseph Smith's profound inquiries, the commandment given was to share the knowledge he had gained with all men and women everywhere.

Each step of the process is an eternal principle. As I see it, the principles involved are stated in the text that follows in the sequential order required to activate the process for discovering that which is true. The principles that govern the process are discussed separately for clarity. However, in application they are almost always used concurrently.

> First, one must have faith sufficient to inaugurate and to sustain the work required to learn.
>
> Second, one must recognize the greater truth and accept it when it is revealed.
>
> Third, one must effectively incorporate the greater understanding into his or her earlier framework of ideas and beliefs; and at the same time one must discard those views that are inconsistent or inaccurate.
>
> Fourth, one must continue the process because understanding is acquired precept by precept.

Faith Sufficient to Activate Work As Needed Is the First Principle

Truth can only be discovered by the individual who has a dynamic faith in its existence and its accessibility. It is possible for each one of us to discern that which is true. However, if we believe we cannot learn, we will not learn. On the other hand, if we believe we can learn and pursue the process vigorously, we will learn. For example, before he left his home port Columbus believed in the probability of reaching the East by sailing west. He believed it sufficiently to persuade the king and queen of Spain to give him some ships. He believed it enough to outfit the ships and recruit crews. He believed in the idea enough to continue to sail west even after he had gone so far out upon the waters that there were no signs of land anywhere. His faith was so dynamic that it persisted even though some of the crew feared that they would soon sail off the edge of the flat surface of the earth. His faith gave mankind a new understanding of the world on which they lived—an understanding far more truthful than most of them had ever known before. This is the kind of faith we need if we are to discover truth.

I do not think it is possible to overstate the importance of cultivating the desire to know what is true. Truth cannot be thrust upon someone. Individuals who do not want to know will not come to new light. Those who think that they already know all things well enough will gain little or no additional understanding. The desire to know should be nurtured from the time one feels the faintest hope or whisper that truth is accessible. It is critically important to do so.

In order to make progress, our belief in the possibility of learning must lead us to select appropriate activities that will prepare us to receive the additional truths we desire. If we are interested in learning about important matters, we can be certain that the work required will be very difficult; we can also know that it will be very satisfying.

The initiatives and hard work of discovering truth almost always include an examination of what is known. This requires achieving competency in the use of the major symbol systems by which men and women communicate ideas. The two fundamental systems are language and mathematics. One needs to know how both systems work and how to use them effectively. This makes it possible to comprehend ideas. Ideas cannot be consciously accepted or rejected if they are not understood. It is interesting that the restoration of the gospel in this dispensation began with a period of general enlightenment not found in previous periods of history. The Bible was taken from the cloistered centers of religious scholarship, translated, and printed for all men and women to read. Further, revelation waited a little longer until there was the beginning of literacy among the people so that they could read the testament of both the Jews and the peoples of the American continent, and compare them.

Often we cannot discover what is unknown or in error unless we carefully study what is known. We need an awareness of the knowledge available if we are to push back the limits of the known and discover what is yet hidden. Certainly this has been true in the various sciences. It has been equally true in efforts to understand the nature of God. The boy Joseph Smith was interested and informed about the religious excitement of his day, and he read diligently in the Bible. A combination of these efforts led him to the prayerful entreaty which brought profound understanding from heaven.

It is not enough to become literate in the basic symbol systems and to become aware of the information and ideas available today. The hard work of study comes as the individual analyzes the parts of the whole, evaluates the propositions posed, and reasons carefully while testing the validity of various arguments and positions. The further steps of study require the individual to synthesize information and impressions into an intelligent proposition which may lead to another effort to gain greater wisdom and enlightenment. In the exciting history of man's search for knowledge, individuals occasionally acquire unexpected insight. This always occurs while they are in the diligent search to understand problems they are actively considering.

It is clear that a specific study may require special activities as the search is pursued. Madame Curie realized she had to carry out difficult, sometimes tedious, laboratory procedures to prepare her to identify a new element and understand its properties. Joseph Smith realized he must appeal to God in searching prayer to prepare himself to understand the truth concerning the nature and purposes of God.

Acceptance of Revelation Is the Second Principle

Revelation is the experience of coming to know a greater or an additional truth through the influence of the Spirit. It is a fulfilling, joyful experience that follows considerable effort. Revelation is the uncovering of a true principle that previously was not open to our view.

Revelation, in a sense, is only a partial experience. All that is true is not given to us in one sweeping, final statement; rather it is obtained little by little through the arduous process of discovery. It is a process we should engage in for a lifetime and more. Some revelations are of incredible importance and the truths understood are profound, but still they are only partial realizations of the whole truth. Each revelatory experience is only one in a sequence that leads toward the ultimate truth.

The Father and His Son Jesus Christ are one in truth. They possess an understanding of all true principles, and it is through them and the opportunities they have made available to us that truth is brought into the world. In attributing the source of truth to the Father and the Son, it is of profound importance to remember that they do not capriciously create truth. They already understand what is true and have arranged a way through which this can be revealed to us.

In the great plan that allows us to pursue the purpose of life, there has been included the influence of the Holy Ghost, a spirit that verifies the truth to us. Revelatory experiences involve the whole being of an individual. The senses, mind, and heart are all involved in the experience of coming to know what is true. Different senses or different aspects of our total capacities dominate in the different kinds of revelatory experiences that we can have. The Holy Spirit is able to work through the prepared soul to bring about the needed realization of truth in a way that is appropriate for the specific truth being learned.

When we vigorously seek truth through the process being described here, we prepare ourselves for the quiet workings of the Spirit, which confirms truth to our souls. It is not sufficient to merely ask for truth.

The Range of Revelatory Experiences

In almost all cases the revelatory experience consists of a peaceful feeling of reassurance that comes into the soul as the Spirit of the Lord acknowledges truth. As we consider the various options in a particular circumstance and search them out in our mind, the option that is most right simply "feels" right. In a real sense, the correctness of the option selected in the struggle to know gives the sensation of light to the mind. Newton explained how, as he kept problems constantly before him, working them out in his mind, truth came first as a ray of light that later opened into the full brightness of day. The quiet, peaceful feeling that comes into the mind and soul is the reassurance of what is true that is vital and can be recognized by those who are experienced in seeking truth.

Occasionally there is a much stronger emotional feeling associated with the experience of coming to know something that is true. This experience is more a difference in degree than a difference in kind. On these occasions the feelings associated with the recognition of truth are more accurately described as a sense of burning within. The one involved can hardly describe to another what has happened, but the experience is so profound that the one who has had it recognizes its importance. The feeling of rightness about what is being considered is associated with the mind and the emotions in such a way that a clear signal is recognized and the one involved knows that he has come closer to truth.

On special occasions, a few who have met the prerequisites for revelation are instructed as though a voice speaks to them in the mind confirming the truthfulness of what was being considered. The very words that describe or state the greater understanding seem to form in the mind and are then immediately transmitted to the soul. Even less often, an audible voice comes to individuals with specific instructions. The voice is heard through the sense of hearing in these extraordinary experiences.

On very special occasions, dreams are experienced that communicate truth. Information is made known to seeking people through the natural process of dreaming, but the experience is extended and changed through the influence of the Spirit. These occasions are rare and are prompted by the special need for information that would not be available to individuals through more regular experiences. Therefore, the searching soul is sometimes blessed with specific communication in such a way that the needed information is made known.

In still fewer cases in the history of the world, God has seen fit to allow mortal beings to see and to converse with someone who has already passed beyond mortality. In such cases the individual messenger, or ''angel,'' is sent to give specific instructions. The messenger may repeat the same instruction more than once to be certain that the instruction is understood. The instruction is so important that it must not only be understood but it must also be impossible to misunderstand.

The most rare revelatory experiences of all have occurred when a seeker has not only prepared appropriately but is selected by God and is allowed to behold an open vision of the Father or the Son Jesus Christ or both. The mortal mission of one given that incredible experience is of such profound importance to the well-being of other people that the one chosen could not carry out this responsibility without being absolutely clear about the very nature of God and the individual's special relationship to Him.

It is important to emphasize that revelatory experiences also extend over the full range of true principles. The intensity of the experience and the significance of the truth are closely related. Coming to any true principle is a revelatory experience. The source is the same. The means of recognition is similar and inspiration is involved even when the recipient is unaware of the source.

Acceptance of the truth revealed is crucial to continuing progress.

There Is a Counterfeit to the Revelatory Experience

Unfortunately there have been experiences in human history where the experience deemed to be revelatory has not been genuine. When credence is given to such counterfeit experiences the cause of truth is not served and progress is blocked.

Most often these experiences come when individuals arouse their own emotional and mental conditions without discipline of minds and feelings. Failure to master the discipline of hard and extensive work in verifying and considering ideas can make one prey to false concepts.

It is appropriate for us to live spiritual lives, lives that are directed and influenced by the Spirit along a path that takes us closer and closer to the truth. This is in direct contrast to living lives that are either self-stimulated, induced by drugs, or intensified by Satan. Any of these sources can stimulate the emotion in what is thought to be a religious experience but truly is not. Furthermore, such undirected and undisciplined feelings divert us from pure truth and make it difficult to discern the influence of the Spirit.

Even the most thoughtful seekers of truth find times when their paths are unclear, when they are required to struggle for an extended period of time before they gain greater truth or resolution of their problem. It is necessary for us to struggle and to extend ourselves in the search over time. It is not easy to learn important things.

There are several principles that are particularly helpful in directing us during these times of struggle and uncertainty. When we are troubled or unsure about the source of our feelings, it is of great benefit to ponder the condition of our heart. It is helpful to test our feelings and thoughts and evaluate our approach to be sure it is consistent with the principles of the process. If not, we can be sure that the influence is not that of the Spirit.

It is also helpful to remember that truths cannot conflict. If uncertainty and questions come about because there is an apparent conflict between true principles, we can be certain that we need to search further. The Spirit only confirms that which is true. If we are considering an option that conflicts with other true principles, the Spirit will not assure us.

Finally, the most important of all guides in helping us evaluate the source of our feelings is to examine the results of the assumed truth when it is applied. Careful observations justify the validity of what we have come to believe. The results of truth will be good and productive.

The Time of the Revelatory Experience Cannot Be Ordered

The influence of the Spirit does not come in a constant high-intensity signal. Though we should always seek truth with intensity and be vigorous in our adherence to the true principles we have come to know, the moments of communication through the Spirit are irregular and sometimes quite separated in time. I feel certain this is because it is of great importance that we be personally responsible for our lives and that we make choices between truth and error.

Our agency and personal responsibility would be lost if there were an external source of evaluation that constantly directed us to do this or to do that. Such loss of responsibility would divert the whole plan for our development in life. Therefore, even if we are constantly seeking truth in an appropriate way, still there will be only occasional experiences of great significance that come to us to direct our path.

Furthermore, we cannot command the Spirit. We are responsible to be accessible to the Spirit at all times. God will discern when and to what extent additional truths should be revealed. From His greater perspective, He selects the time of need and purpose. Perhaps the following analysis will help make this more clear.

In recent years scientists have learned a great deal about our distant sister planet, Saturn. Exciting new information has been transmitted to earth via spacecraft in a very special way. To appreciate this incredible accomplishment it is necessary to know several important facts. Both the planet and the spacecraft (the source of the information) were approximately 930,000,000 miles away from earth at the time of observation. Even though the signal from the satellite traveled at the speed of light, 186,000 miles per second, it took one and one-half hours for the information to travel from the satellite to the earth. The power available to send the signal from the satellite was only one-eighth of one watt. That signal was so weak that it would take an 85-foot-diameter antenna 67 million years to gather enough energy to light a seven-and-a-half-watt night lamp for a mere thousandth of a second. Many other natural signals caused a background noise far more energetic than the signal from the spacecraft. Therefore, the scientists were faced with a very difficult problem. The detailed information collected by the satellite had to be transmitted by very low power over vast distances in such a way that a specially prepared receiver could detect a signal and interpret the information. The task was successfully accomplished. First, the signal was coded so that the information was sent in a changing signal. The variations in the signal allowed detection, whereas a constant source would not. A doorbell ringing all the time tells you less than one that rings only when someone comes to call.

The Spirit seems to communicate more directly at the moment new truth is being learned or when we are threatened with falsehood. When we are acting in harmony with truth, no additional signal is needed. If we know the code, we can accurately sort out the signal, even though it is weak, from all the varying, competing signals. The detector, if properly tuned and directed to the source, can record the signal. Other receivers not tuned or not properly directed can receive the signal but can never differentiate it from the noise. Having recorded the signal and knowing how it will be different from other sometimes stronger signals, one can isolate and decode it through sophisticated screening techniques. In this way, analogous with the signal from the spacecraft, a new truth can be made known to man concerning another of God's creations.

Appropriate Change Is the Third Principle

When we receive revelation we are responsible to

incorporate the greater understanding into our framework of ideas and beliefs. Sometimes this means we must add concepts; sometimes it means we must discard views that are inconsistent or inaccurate; and, sometimes, in fact most often, it means a combination of both.

When additional understanding is revealed and we are in possession of greater truth, we are responsible to change our thoughts and actions to conform to the greater truth. The process of discovering true principles cannot continue unless we constantly modify our thoughts and applications, making them consistent with all that has been made known.

Self-directed change toward truth brings harmony into our thoughts and actions. It extends the circle of our understanding and helps us identify the next set of questions to be studied and resolved. Without appropriate change, progress is stopped. The process cannot continue.

Continuing the Process Is the Fourth Principle

Since we are capable of coming to truth only in successive approximations, it is essential that we continue the search. If we are to accomplish our purpose in mortality, life must be an unending quest for that which is true.

The greatest challenge we face in continuing the process of acquiring truth is to recognize that it is difficult to learn. The pursuit of truth often becomes even more difficult as the simpler problems are studied and understood. Additional understanding on the subject comes only after even greater effort.

Another challenge is to pursue that which is true over a wide range of subjects. It is common for us to be open and engage the process in one part of our quest for truth and refuse to even consider the importance of engaging the same kind of search in another. A fine scientist might successfully pursue the path toward the true principles that govern part of God's creation but never agree to

pursue the same process with the same intensity in search
of an understanding of God or the purpose of life. An im-
balance develops, and a limitation comes to those whose
search for truth is distorted in this way.

Yet another challenge in the process is the requirement to keep proper relationship and perspective between
principles. As we learn, we often become frustrated because some concepts we have advocated vigorously are
brought into question. We sense that we must change or
qualify an earlier view, and this is unsettling. Often we
find that more than one principle must be considered
simultaneously. In some cases one of the principles may
dominate and in other cases another principle may become more significant. It is common to find that both
principles must be applied at the same time.

The challenge is illustrated in this example. Some
view the world as operating totally by chance, devoid of
divine influence. Others believe that God is interceding in
everything and that all of us are constrained by His influence without the capability of determining the outcome of
our lives. Neither extreme is accurate. We are responsible
to learn and to make choices. We are responsible for our
choices, and they have a great bearing on our lives. God
can and does influence and intervene in our lives in special
situations and in ways that are consistent with truth and
His greater understanding. He protects for us our right to
choose.

When we do allow that it may be important to pursue other areas of truth, we sometimes impose conditions
that violate the very laws which govern the process of acquiring greater truth. We might say, "When it has been
fully proved, I will consider it." No true principle could
ever be uncovered if all scientists took this position. The
full experiment must be performed. No human being will
come to understand his relationship to God this way,
either. The full pattern given by God must be followed.

The principles that govern the discovery of truth always lead to success. The principles do not change with time. They work whether one is trying to learn arithmetic, quantum mechanics, or the nature of God. The outcome does not always match our desire or our time frame; yet, progress is always made, and after struggle, greater understanding does come.

As we pursue the process of learning we are protected from departing from that which is true. We can constantly observe the results; we can tell whether they are good or bad. A greater truth concerning nature will allow us to predict more accurately the events we observe. A greater truth applied in the way we treat others will provide them with opportunity, and it will bring about in us a sense of happiness and peace. The further we depart from truth, the more obvious the error and the less peace we feel.

Part Two

On Understanding the Family of God

Chapter Four

‖ The Family of God Exists

It seems to me that the most significant truth—the truth that gives purpose and meaning to everything else—is the truth that sets forth the nature and relationship of God and man. No idea I have ever contemplated and pondered in my heart has given me a greater sense of wonder and humility than the truth revealed again concerning the familial relationships which exist between God and man, between God and Jesus Christ, between Jesus Christ and man, and between the people of this world. I am convinced that one's acceptance or rejection of these relationships will make all the difference in how one lives his or her life.

The Existence of a Family of God Is Revealed

There is a great family of individual beings who, like truth, have always existed and will always exist.

The Patriarch of this family of beings is God. He is our Eternal Father.

Jesus Christ is the Only Begotten Son of God. He is the elder brother of all men and women. By special assignment He is the Savior of mankind. All men and women who have come or will come to this earth are sons and daughters of God and brothers and sisters of Jesus Christ and of each other.

Satan and his associates were once part of the family of God, but because they chose to violate true principles they are now estranged from the family.

The Nature of God, Our Eternal Father

God exists.
He is a perfected, corporeal being.
He is perfect in truth and in love.
He is knowable.

God Exists

The fundamental fact, it seems to me, is that God exists. His existence is quite independent of either our perception of Him or of our acknowledgment of Him. It is possible for us to deny ourselves the benefit of this knowledge. It is not possible for us to deny God His existence.

The significance of this understanding is much like the significance of understanding that truth exists. It means we begin with the belief and through the process of seeking for confirmation we come to know God. The knowledge that He lives gives peace and purpose to our lives. In my judgment the realization that He is literally our Eternal Father adds a significant dimension to the value and potential of each human life.

God Is a Perfected, Corporeal Being

Our Eternal Father is a corporeal being. He is neither an essence nor a formless spirit, although His influence extends throughout the universe. He has a soul comprised of a spirit, and a body of flesh and bone. He has emotions and at least all of the senses with which we are familiar.

We are made in His image, and therefore we know that His appearance is like ours.

Our Heavenly Father and Jesus Christ are separate, distinct individuals. Both have always existed. They are one in truth and one in purpose. That is, they have both mastered all true principles and they are completely united in their efforts to use these principles to serve the children of God. They both have godly attributes; but they are not part of the same essence or spirit. One of the remarkable insights into the nature of God given the world through modern revelation is paraphrased: as man is, God once was, and as God is, man may become. It has been revealed that God our Eternal Father has been through a process that brought Him to His state of godliness. He has been successful in the process of perfecting His soul and therefore has achieved His extraordinary state. He has become perfect in wisdom and in love and this is the source of His great power.

The details of when and how and where this development occurred are not known. Knowing that He did engage the struggle of coming to know and understand truth and then of learning to use it to bless other people in perfect charity tells us something significant about the possibility of following His commandments and struggling to become more and more as He is.

God Is Perfect in Truth and in Love

The most significant attributes of our Eternal Father, we are told by revelation, are His wisdom and His love. Our Eternal Father is perfect in both of these attributes, and they encompass all other virtues. He understands all truth in priority and this gives Him wisdom. His glory is His intelligence. Wisdom is prerequisite to being perfect in love. The pure love of God is the most divine of all attributes.

Our Eternal Father has developed an unconditional love or charity for all. His whole motive is to provide opportunity for others, doing for them what they cannot do for themselves and thus leading them forward toward perfection.

Our Eternal Father has developed complete integrity. All that He says and does is consistent with truth. He has perfect control over His emotions. In all situations His emotions are governed by true principles. His integrity, like His compassion, justice, and sympathy, is the result of His perfect wisdom and His perfect love.

He cares about all of us. He knows us individually and is aware of our strengths and our challenges. He has a special purpose for our being here. He does help and influence us in ways consistent with true governing principles. He does not manipulate or force His will upon us.

God's great power and freedom lie in the attributes of the soul that He has developed. This lets us understand that godliness is not another kind of essence. Rather, it is a state of perfection of the soul. Godliness is an acquired state and is achieved when an individual has become perfect.

God Is Knowable

God exists in space and time; therefore, it is possible to come to know God. To do this we must begin and we must endure in a demanding process of developing godliness in our own souls. Our Eternal Father is committed to helping us succeed in the process of coming to know Him. Indeed, His very work is to bring to pass this kind of development for His children. However, we must initiate and maintain an active effort if the development is to be successful.

Simple faith leads us to a beginning understanding of our Eternal Father. To know Him fully we must be like Him. It is not possible for us to truly know a compassionate soul if we have no compassion. It is not possible to know a being filled with truth if we are ignorant or if we are indulging in error. It is not possible for us to know righteousness if we are evil. To know our Eternal Father completely we must develop similar attributes. Though He is incalculably superior, in time we can become like Him and therefore know Him. His work and His glory require that we be able to become like Him and thus ultimately know Him.

Many of the questions we may have concerning God at this time are not yet answered. As we understand what is known we will be given more knowledge. We can come to an understanding of Him only a little at a time. Nevertheless, the possibility to learn more always exists, and that is of profound importance.

The Nature of Jesus Christ

Jesus Christ exists.
He is also a God.
He is a perfected, corporeal being.
He has been resurrected.
He is perfect in love and in truth.
He is knowable.

Jesus Christ Exists

Like God and truth, Jesus Christ exists. He has an existence independent of the mind of man. As noted before in the sections on truth and on God the Eternal Father, the fact that Jesus Christ exists is significant because it offers to the one who believes and accepts this truth a magnificent vision of the eternal nature of life.

Jesus Christ Is a God

Jesus Christ is the Son of God but He is also a God, for He has progressed to the state of godliness by coming to understand all truth, by bringing His life into harmony with that truth, and by using that truth to give love to all. Jesus Christ became a God before he came to earth.

Though a separate being from the Father, he is one in purpose, one in love, and one in truth. During an earlier age He was successful in the process of perfecting His spirit and therefore achieved the status of godhood.

Jesus Christ Is a Perfected, Corporeal Being

Jesus Christ has a perfected spirit and a perfected body now united eternally. He is in form like us and He has the emotional responses we know. He has the qualities of the soul which we recognize as being the foundation of character. He is a perfected man.

Jesus Christ Has Been Resurrected

Jesus Christ is a resurrected being who lives again after death. As the "first fruits" of the Resurrection, Jesus Christ's reappearance to many men and women in the flesh gives us assurance not only that He lives but also that He lives as a perfected man.

Jesus Christ Is Knowable

Like the Father, Jesus Christ exists in time and place and can be known by men and women. By becoming more wise and more loving we become more like Christ and therefore we know Him better.

The Nature of Mankind

Mankind (meaning men and women) exists.

Men and women are beings of body, parts, and passions.

Men and women are imperfect.

Men and women are coeternal with God. Intelligence is one of the eternal realities that cannot be created or made.

Men and women are the spirit children of God the
Eternal Father and as such are of the race of the
gods with the potential of godliness.

Men and women are brothers and sisters of Jesus
Christ and of each other.

Mankind (Men and Women) Exists

Individually all people have an existence independent of what they or others choose to believe.

Like God and Jesus Christ, each person has a body
which exists in time and place and is not the figment of
imagination.

Men and Women Are Beings of Body, Parts, and Passions

Men and women have both bodies and spirits. Together, the body and the spirit make up the soul.

They have emotions.

They experience life through their minds and their
senses.

Men and Women Are Imperfect

Men and women are mortal, which means that
neither their bodies nor their spirits are perfected. Further
it means that body and spirit will be separated through
death.

Men and Women Are Coeternal with God

Through revelation we understand that all of us
have forever coexisted with God as intelligence. Intelligence is one of the eternal realities that cannot be created
or made. Intelligence, which is the eternal core of each person, is something which has always existed.

Men and Women Are the Spirit Offspring of God

Men and women are the literal spirit offspring of God the Eternal Father and as such have a birthright which makes them capable of becoming as He is. Understanding these eternal relationships gives us a responsibility to strive to develop appropriate warm, loving, nurturing feelings toward our Heavenly Father and toward each other. The relationships are so significant that they enlarge our understanding to an appreciation of the ongoing nature of human life, and to an exciting view of our potential.

Men and Women Are Brothers and Sisters

All men and women are children in the family of God. Jesus Christ is our elder brother. Recognizing that we have and always will have this relationship with each other motivates us to treat one another differently. Even though some individuals may be very limited in understanding or ability and capable of great evil, they have the potential to rise above their present condition. Every soul is capable of enlargement through repentance of evil, correction of error, and vigorous searching for continued enlightenment. Every one is a brother and sister and must be viewed with respect. Because Jesus Christ, our elder brother, has achieved the state of godliness as our Father has and has provided unlimited opportunities for us, He deserves our deepest respect, admiration, and love. We are to follow after Him.

The Nature of Those Estranged from God Is Known

These are also the children of God. Most of them have no bodies.

Satan (Lucifer) is the leader of those estranged from God.

Those Estranged Are Children of God

Beings who are estranged from God are children of God who made choices that took them away from their Eternal Father. Their leader is Satan, also a son of God, but one motivated by selfishness. He chose not to achieve power and freedom through living in harmony with true principles.

Most Estranged Beings Have No Bodies

Most estranged beings have spirit bodies but no mortal bodies. Their choices in violation of true principles have led them to a condition in which their opportunities are greatly limited.

Some who are estranged received mortal bodies, gained conviction of many true principles, including a knowledge of Christ, and then denied Him. These beings also are estranged from God and are led by Satan.

Chapter Five

Some Revealed Responsibilities of Our Eternal Father, Jesus Christ, and Mankind

Through revelation given to His prophets both anciently and in modern times, our Eternal Father has explained to us the purpose of life and our individual responsibilities toward accomplishing that purpose. This understanding is the light which He promised and which, I believe, makes a meaningful existence possible.

Because of our divine nature as the literal children of God, our Eternal Father, we all have the capacity to become perfect even as He is perfect. This quest is the purpose of life. God, Jesus Christ, and mankind have responsibilities in bringing to pass this universal opportunity for personal perfection.

Some Known Responsibilities of God Our Eternal Father

God our Eternal Father presides over His family and is responsible to provide for all of His children an opportunity to achieve their full potential. He is responsible to provide truth and charitable love in the way that will encourage His children to continue their struggle toward perfection.

God became the father of our spirits and is responsible to preside over the family. He became responsible to provide for all of His children an opportunity to achieve their full potential; therefore, He established His plan of salvation, which makes it possible for His children to progress without limits until they accomplish the purpose of life.

The most important part of the plan was initiated when our Eternal Father designated His eldest son, Jesus Christ, to become the Savior of mankind. Our Eternal Father has declared that His central responsibility is to help His children succeed in accomplishing the purpose of life.

Our Eternal Father constantly watches over us and gives us light and knowledge and encouragement sufficient to allow us to continue our progress toward perfection. This means that He will initiate such actions as He sees necessary to make it possible for us to choose good and overcome evil in our lives. If we turn to Him, seeking, we can avail ourselves of His strength and compassion.

Some Known Responsibilities of Jesus Christ

Under the direction of our Eternal Father, Jesus Christ was responsible to

— Create the earth, the heavens, and all living things on the earth.

— Teach true principles to the inhabitants of the earth from the beginning of mortality.

— Participate in the mortal experience in order to provide an example of a perfect life for all mankind to follow.

— Give up His life on earth willingly and be resurrected, thus atoning for our sins and making it possible for all mankind to overcome their errors and death and acquire a perfected resurrected body after death.

– Teach true principles to those who have died.

– Return to the earth a second time to preside over His church and to complete His work of providing truth and opportunity to our Heavenly Father's children (His brothers and sisters).

Because Jesus Christ was qualified, and because He understood and lived in perfect harmony with true principles, He was selected to be the Savior of mankind and thus to carry out our Eternal Father's plan.

Therefore, acting under the direction of His Father, He created the earth and the heavens. Knowing the true governing principles and using the materials already available, He organized this place where our development could occur. The culminating creative responsibility was to organize the physical bodies for the spirit children of God.

Jesus Christ's next great responsibility was to teach the inhabitants of the earth true principles in order to make it possible for them to accomplish their purpose in coming here. He carried out this responsibility as Jehovah, the teacher of mankind, before the advent of His mortal ministry.

Jesus Christ was then responsible to accomplish another critical part of His assigned work as a participant in the mortal experience. He was the promised Messiah. He had a unique birth and life here. God the Eternal Father is the father of Jesus Christ's mortal body in addition to being the father of His spirit. Furthermore, Jesus Christ matured without violating a single true principle. He provided the children of God a perfect example of godliness in mortal conditions. He taught true principles by word and by example.

Jesus Christ was also responsible to sacrifice himself for us. Because of His unique divine nature, He had power over death and the ability to fulfill the requirements of eternal law. He willingly suffered for our sins, gave His life, and came forth from the tomb in order to make it possible for us to overcome our sins, to live again after death, and to be united with a resurrected body.

Jesus Christ is now a resurrected being. He is a living testament to the truth that life is eternal.

Jesus Christ continues His responsibility to teach true principles to the inhabitants of the earth and to those who have gone on through death, and to direct His church. He reveals truth to His prophets for the people as a whole and to individuals who seek for personal light. He will return to the earth as a resurrected being to take personal charge of His church and to personally direct the teaching of the gospel to the people of the world. This responsibility will not end until every child of God has had full opportunity to learn and accept true principles, which will allow them to perfect themselves, and until mankind has learned to subdue the earth by discovering the principles upon which it operates.

Some Known Responsibilities of Mankind

All mankind are principal participants in the great plan of our Eternal Father, which has been implemented by Jesus Christ. Because of their wisdom and love, the Father and the Son have done for us what we are not capable of doing for ourselves. However, that which we can do we are responsible to do.

> We were responsible to choose whether to participate in the great plan and to assume the challenges of this mortal experience.
>
> We are now responsible to take full advantage of the opportunity provided for us here in mortality to pursue the purpose of life.
>
> We have a responsibility to struggle to understand all true principles and to live in harmony with the truth that we know.

|| We have a responsibility to perfect ourselves in
|| our ability to give love.

Although we are unable to control every event or
condition in life, we are able to control many events, and
without exception we can control whether the circumstances of our lives contribute to our progress or take us
away from our ultimate goal. We are responsible to engage
life from the perspective that all challenges can give us
experiences in choosing truth and developing love.

We must assume full responsibility for determining
the outcome of our lives. Divine influence can help us in
our efforts, but we must prepare ourselves in order to gain
this help.

We are responsible to engage the process that leads
to greater truth. We are responsible to change the way we
think, feel, and act until our lives are consistent with the
truth we have learned. Finally, we are responsible to continue in this process of learning and loving until we have
perfected our souls.

The Condition of Those Estranged
from the Family of God

|| Lucifer leads those spirits who followed him and
|| are now unable to progress. They seek to entice
|| others to walk with them in darkness.

Lucifer, once one of our Father's very successful
sons, denied himself the opportunity to contribute to the
work of our Eternal Father; therefore, he has no responsibilities or authority. However, he and his associates have
taken it upon themselves to entice others to fail in the quest
for eternal life.

These who do not have the opportunity to progress
toward perfection are in their miserable state because they
persisted in contradicting known principles of truth.

Chapter Six

The History and Future of the Family of God

The concept of eternity is one of the very profound contributions which God has made to our understanding. Acceptance of the idea that there is no beginning and no end comes very slowly to men and women, perhaps because of our experience with and observation of birth and death.

It seems to me that God has made us aware of the concept of eternity in order to help us understand the purpose of life. This concept allows us to see beyond our limited experience and to recognize that birth and death are endings of life in one condition and the beginnings of life in another. As such they are transitions.

The study of nonliving things frequently leads to observations of dramatic changes in their condition. A nuclear explosion, for example, marks the transition of complex atoms into simpler, more tightly bound atoms. In the transition, mass energy is transformed into other forms of energy. We are awed by the effects of the change. In all such cases something is continued through the transitions even if the forms are very different. God has made it known that there is continuity through transitions for living things as well. For all men and women, individual identity continues through the transitions of birth and death. Without this understanding of eternity, it is impossible to understand the purpose of life.

God has explained our purpose in life in terms of

continual progress toward perfection. The nature of eternal existence makes reasonable this sense of ongoing development before birth, in mortality, and after death.

Let us now consider what is known of the history and future of the family of God in terms of these three time periods. This brief statement of the past and future of mankind's existence has come to us through the revelations of God and provides what seems to me to be a critically important dimension to our understanding of the current and past record of mankind's earthly experience. These revelations let us see the master plan of salvation which God has prepared to allow His children to find success in achieving the purpose of mortal life.

The Premortal Period of Life

|| This is the period of time which precedes the experience on earth for the children of God.

The essential events of the premortal period have been revealed as follows: all of us coexisted with God; intelligence is one of the eternal realities that cannot be created or destroyed.

I believe one of the most significant revelations ever given is the explanation that as man is, God once was, and as God is, man may become. Before this world began God succeeded in perfecting Himself.

Also in this period, before we were born into mortality, we came into the family of God as His spirit children. By the work of God the Eternal Father, intelligence took on spirit form.

We did not all develop at the same rate during the premortal interval. Individually we made choices and progressed. Some became noble and great and were given conditional assignments to assume responsible roles in the mortal experience which was to follow. For example, the scriptures testify that Abraham was among those that were noble and great, and Jeremiah was ordained a prophet before he was born. The ordination gave Jeremiah the opportunity to serve. Still, he had to live a life in mortality worthy of the assignment. He was foreordained to specific responsibilities in mortality but not predestined to carry them out.

Like all the children of God, Jesus Christ coexisted with the Father. He was a separate being before He was born to Mary in mortality.

Jesus Christ, the most successful of all our Father's children, became a spirit child of God during premortal time just as all of His brothers and sisters did. He also became a God before He came in the flesh. As He became godly, He became "one" with our Eternal Father—one in truth, one in love, and one in purpose.

In a great council of all His spirit children, God the Father outlined the plan of salvation. He explained its essential elements, including the need for agency and personal choice.

In this great council the Father sought a volunteer to become the savior of mankind. One, named Lucifer, arose and agreed to take on the task but only on his own terms: that he be allowed to force all to return to the presence of God, and thus honor and glory would be his. This plan was not in harmony with eternal principles and God chose another for this important work. He designated His Firstborn Son, whom we know as Jesus Christ, to be the Savior of mankind and to carry out the atoning sacrifice. Jesus Christ also volunteered for this work, giving all the honor and the glory to the Father and agreeing to do the work in the context of eternal laws and principles. This preserves for individual spirits the right of choice or agency.

Eventually, approximately one-third of the spirit children of God chose to follow Lucifer. This decision prevented them from having a body, and this stopped their eternal progress. The rest of the children of God decided to accept the risks and and rewards of mortality.

Jesus Christ, in His new role and under the direction of the Eternal Father, created the world by organizing existing matter and preparing the earth and the heavens as the environment in which men and women could come for their earthly experiences. The Creation was not accomplished by chance. Neither was the Creation brought about from nothing. Jesus Christ took from those materials that already existed and organized them in harmony with eternal laws and principles. His knowledge of truth made this possible. This creation was an act of grace or love because He did for us what we could not do for ourselves.

The final act of creation was to organize physical bodies for Adam and Eve. This act also was accomplished in harmony with law. Adam became the first of the spirit children of God to come to earth and to be given a body. Eve's body was also created and joined with her spirit in order to make the full plan possible.

Jesus Christ, as the Jehovah of early scriptures, continued His responsibilities as teacher of mankind. During this time, consistent with the purpose of the Creation, He taught true principles to Adam and Eve and their descendents. In every age when mortals would allow, He has revealed true principles to the prophets. Without this knowledge mankind could not make the choices that would give them the possibility of succeeding in the purpose of life.

The premortal period ends at different times for different spirits, but the end comes in essentially the same way for all who enter a mortal body. All leave the heavenly place where they have been dwelling with their Eternal Father to be born on earth. The birth for each individual is entrance into mortality through a veil of forgetfulness which deprives us of memory of the events of the premortal time but opens the way to continued progress.

The Mortal Period of Life Is Consciously Experienced

The mortal period begins with birth and ends with death. It is the short period of time best known to men and women, for it is the extent of their rememberable experience.

Although we made the choice to become mortal beings, each of us entered the period of mortality without memory of the great events of the premortal experience. The reason for this lack of ready consciousness of the past is that true principles of growth require that we be free to make individual choices in an educational experience, allowing us to pursue understanding of true principles and incorporate them into our lives by choice without the direct influence of the Father and of Jesus Christ. This is the essential ingredient of the educational experience which we know as mortality. The beginning of mortality for each of the spirit children of God is known as birth. All of the spirits who elected to participate have been or will be provided with an opportunity to come to earth to mortal bodies.

The concluding part of the work of creation was to provide the mortal bodies. In order to do this the Eternal Father and Jesus Christ brought Adam, then Eve, into a place of transition called the Garden of Eden. Here they were instructed that the garden was for their use, except they were not to eat of the tree of knowledge of good and evil, which would enable them to discern good from evil and make them subject to mortal death. They were also instructed to multiply and replenish the earth. In the extreme, these two instructions seem incompatible, but I am confident that as we gain more understanding of the principles involved and the symbols used, all will be resolved. Adam and Eve had to participate in the decision to become separated from God, and they had to be responsible for what they did. The choices were made. Adam and Eve partook of the forbidden fruit and became fully mortal. It was a necessary step to provide the opportunity of mortal life for all of God's children.

We are self-oriented as babies, incapable of responding to the needs of others. Tiny babies do not cry when other babies are hungry; they cry when they themselves are hungry. Nevertheless, all babies are free from sin. Our birth into mortality is not intrinsically the result of transgression. We are capable of learning and then choosing, and it is upon our own choices that our progress in eternal things depends.

Each individual has access to the influence of the Spirit, which, as has been explained, confirms truth to the soul which seeks.

The experiences of mortality make it possible for each of us individually to make great progress in our ultimate goal of becoming like Jesus Christ and our Eternal Father. During this period of time each soul may respond to the challenges of his or her individual circumstances in such a way as to learn true principles, to exercise wisdom, and to develop and to practice charitable love.

We leave mortality by the process of death, which is a temporary separation of the body and the spirit that inaugurates our participation in the events of the postmortal period.

One of the truly monumental events of the mortal period was the personal ministry of Jesus Christ. It was part of the eternal plan that Jesus Christ would spend an interval in mortality to teach by example and to perform the great atoning sacrifice.

Jesus Christ had a divine birth. In a way not completely understood by man, but I believe in harmony with eternal natural laws, the Savior was brought into a mortal existence. His mortal mother was Mary, a virgin, and His father was God, the Eternal Father. Thus Jesus Christ entered mortality different from all others. He was born of a mortal mother and thus could know death; and He was born of a divine Father and thus could conquer death. He brought with Him elements of His godly nature that none of us possesses.

He matured in mortality, developing His full capacity as a part-mortal being. He went through a process of development in a way similar to that of any other child. He increased in stature as His body matured into adulthood. He also increased in wisdom as He asked questions searching for truth and as He was asked questions by others. In this state He again came to know true principles. As He did so, he also increased in grace, or the capacity to love, until the full grace of God came upon Him. This growing process is an important element in the example provided. It is of great consequence for us to observe that even the Savior increased in truth and grace, or wisdom and love, in steps. He did not have the fulness at the first of His mortality, but proceeded to the fulness by succeeding in this process. Although He matured in mortality, He did not transgress eternal law. Therefore, He was free from sin. In this way His development was unique. He is the only one on this earth who has lived a perfect life—that is, He has lived without yielding to the temptation to violate true principles.

The mature Christ provided for us a perfect example. He showed us in our own environment what it means to be godly. He was, and is, the truth, the light, and the way. It was imperative that He personally illustrate the perfect life by His own example. Understanding the needs of His brothers and sisters and understanding the truth in proper priority, He is capable of treating us with a perfect love. His whole mortal experience motivated by love was an act of grace. He chose to participate in this difficult experience. Because of our need and the requirements of eternal law, He pursued the same purposes here that had

motivated His acts of grace during His premortal state. We
have record of true principles He taught as Jehovah. He
taught even more true principles as Jesus of Nazareth.

The most critical part of the entire plan was for
Jesus Christ to allow His mortal state to come to an end by
offering Himself as a perfect sacrifice in order to end the
separation of mankind from God. It has been revealed that
this selfless act by the Christ was necessary to satisfy
justice and to make it possible for mankind to overcome
the separation from God.

In the work of the Atonement, Jesus Christ made
possible the resurrection, which overcomes death and
allows the body and the spirit to be reunited eternally. The
Atonement also makes it possible to overcome the separation caused by sin through the process of repentance.

The Atonement, like the Creation, and like the
mortal life of Jesus Christ, was an act of grace. Christ's
love was made possible by His knowledge of all truth. He
performed for us essential acts which we could not perform for ourselves.

In harmony with laws not yet understood, Christ
rose from the tomb. Three days after the Crucifixion He
again took up His physical body and became a perfect,
resurrected being. In this new state He continued to teach
true principles to the Apostles and to others as He had
been doing since He was assigned work as the Savior
before the world was. He accomplished the literal fulfillment of prophecy. He showed the disciples that the individual soul—a being of body, parts, passions, and a spirit
—continues after death. He made it clear that He was not
merely a spiritual symbol, but, in fact, a living being.
Christ's coming forth from the tomb as a perfect being is
central to our understanding of His work as our Savior.

Coming to earth to receive a body and to make the
commitment to living by true principles no matter the consequence is the essential element of mankind's mortal
experience.

The work of teaching by example in the condition of mortality and the sacred work of the Atonement were the essential events of Jesus Christ's participation in mortality.

The Postmortal Period of Life Is Revealed

The great assurance of revelation is that all mankind will rise from the dead and continue in their eternal existence. This uncircumscribed period of time which follows death is the postmortal period of eternal life.

All individuals who have had and who will have mortal bodies enter into the postmortal period of life by death. All mankind will be resurrected because of the atoning sacrifice of Jesus Christ.

The great message of hope which this knowledge gives is the realization that men and women will retain their individual identity forever and that they may know one another after death and continue their loving and meaningful relationships. It means each child of God may continue to progress eternally.

The great atoning act of Jesus Christ overcame death. Of the act itself we know this much: for three days after the crucifixion of Christ, His body lay in the tomb. He then arose from the dead and left the tomb. He was the first to be resurrected. When He arose from the dead, the righteous who slept also came forth from their tombs.

He showed himself to many: first to Mary in the garden, then to His disciples, and later to His "other sheep" on the American continent. Since then He has appeared to selected prophets to assure mankind that His resurrection has occurred and to continue to teach eternal truths.

When men and women die, their spirits are separated from their bodies. For a time, these spirits reside in a special place called the spirit world. Those individuals who have been more successful in the purpose of life will proceed to a part of the spirit world called "paradise." Those less successful are confined to a "spirit prison." In the spirit world, Jesus Christ and His followers provide instruction. Our Eternal Father has provided this additional opportunity for true principles to be taught so that the inequities of mortality are overcome and everyone will finally have complete access to all true principles and will be able to make those choices that will determine his or her future. During this interval, compensation is made for any lack of opportunity in mortality.

Those who are wicked reside in the spirit prison where they experience the "hell" of knowing that they are responsible for the separation brought about by their own choices to violate truth. Hell then becomes that constant torment known by the wicked, who must finally accept that their own actions have brought them the limitation they experience.

A resurrection will take place for each individual that has lived on earth. This resurrection results in the creation of an immortal soul. In this event the spirit is united with a perfected body that is not subject to death. This perfected body will be complete with all of its parts.

The resurrection will occur in stages. Jesus Christ was the first to be resurrected. He literally came forth from the tomb. Some others who lived and died before Christ came forth from the grave at the time He was resurrected. Some few who died after Christ's resurrection have also been resurrected. Among them are Peter and James, two of Christ's Apostles. All others who are righteous, those who have been successful in mortality and in the spirit world, will be resurrected on the day of the second coming of the Savior to the world. This resurrection is known as the "morning of the first resurrection" and will occur for those who have achieved a celestial state. That is, those who have succeeded in the ultimate purposes of life will be resurrected at the beginning of the Millennium. After the Millennium has begun, those who are good but not godly will be resurrected. Ultimately, at the end of the Millennium, all others will receive immortal bodies to clothe their immortal spirits. The resurrection is universal for all who live on earth. In every case the quality of spirit acquired before resurrection will continue in the resurrected being. The knowledge one has acquired will also rise with the individual.

It is important to stress the fact that there is a direct correlation between the opportunities in the hereafter and one's progress in mortal life. The resurrection will lead to different states. Opportunities available after the resurrection are dependent upon the progress made before the resurrection.

The celestial (or eternal) resurrection provides the greatest opportunity and will be provided for those who have begun to develop godly attributes in their souls. Celestial beings will participate in the creative work of love yet to be accomplished. They will be in the presence of our Eternal Father and Jesus Christ, and they will also be in company with others of their families who have qualified by their personal choices for the celestial work.

The terrestrial resurrection provides significant opportunity. It is for those who lived and died without law and those who are honorable but have not chosen eternal life with the Father and the responsibilities such a choice implies.

The third state is the telestial resurrection. Those who are resurrected into the telestial condition will be those who have not lived honorable lives and who did not accept the truths of the gospel either on earth or in the spirit world.

There will be a few who have had clear testimonies of Jesus Christ, who have known the truth and the power of it but were overcome by their own transgressions and so defiled the power of God for their own supposed personal advantage. These who have known and then denied the spirit of witness will live in darkness and misery with Lucifer and his associates.

The Plan of Salvation

Simply stated the plan of salvation as revealed to mankind is this: The spirit children of God would leave His presence by their own free choice in order to take a necessary step in their continued development toward perfection.

In order to continue to grow, individuals must have the experience of the mortal environment in which they can develop the attributes of godliness. They must learn to walk by faith, to consider the principles of truth as taught by Jesus Christ, and to choose whether to live by those principles. It is also necessary for eternal progression that the spirit be joined with a body which in the resurrection becomes a permanent uniting of the body and the spirit.

The mortal experience makes it possible for the spirit to have a body. It also provides the environment in which agency may be manifest to properly develop faith in Christ and His attributes. There are countless opportunities given to each individual to choose to apply the fundamental message from heaven: namely, learning and loving.

After death the process continues as men and women move forward in their quest for perfection.

Basically the plan provides opportunity for individuals to choose to continue their eternal progress. The key commandments require us to learn truth and then to apply truth in loving service as we have known the Eternal Father and His Son Jesus Christ to do.

It is also important to understand that the judgments of heaven are all made in accordance with the eternal principles which govern and which have been taught from the beginning.

There is no end to the progress that men and women can make. There is no end to the postmortal period.

Part Three

On
Pursuing
the Purpose
of Life

Chapter Seven

Wisdom, Love, and the Purpose of Life

It seems clear to me as I study the scriptures that the divine intent in mortality is a meaningful experience for each of the spirit children of God.

Sometimes, in fact often, the limitations of unperfected body and spirit create situations, circumstances, and experiences that seem devoid of purpose and full of pain. Nevertheless, the work of teaching the truth and uncovering new understanding of the harmony in all truth needs to go on. As it does one can focus on the purpose of life.

> The purpose of life is to learn true principles and to apply them properly in charitable love for everyone.

Through loving application of what is known—following the fundamental instructions from God to do for others what they cannot do for themselves in order to facilitate their progress—the individual slowly begins to make progress in the perfection of his or her own soul.

As we strive to follow the examples given by the Eternal Father and His Son Jesus Christ, it is important to understand what the characteristics of godliness or perfection really are.

By far the most significant characteristics of godliness are wisdom and love. All other virtues either derive from these or are closely related to them.

The Nature of Wisdom

The proper application of true principles requires more than the correct understanding of individual principles. It requires wisdom.

> To have the wisdom of God, we must understand all true principles and keep them in proper relationship to each other in all situations.

To use true principles in a godly way it is necessary to hold all applicable principles in mind at once. It is also necessary to correctly sort out the priority of the principles so that in the composite nature of things the proper perspective is known. This is wisdom, and it allows thoughts and actions that bring about opportunities and results that are good. This wisdom is an attribute of godliness that can be developed.

The Nature of Charity, the Pure Love of Christ

Prophets of all ages have stressed the prime importance of charity, or the pure love of Christ. I have come to appreciate the overriding importance of this great quality as the foundation of godliness. Further, I am beginning to realize that there is a dimension of learning which comes only in the living of true principles.

> The most important attribute for us to develop is pure love or charity. To have charity we must know that which is true, but to know truth without charity is of limited eternal worth.
>
> To love as God loves we must understand the needs of others, understand the true principles that apply in the situation, understand the proper priority of both needs and true principles, and then act, think, and feel in such a way as to

> provide maximum opportunities for others to
> improve themselves as a result of what is done.
>
> Charity for others is the source of the greatest and
> most enduring happiness that can be experienced.

Charity is the dominant element in the character of
God. This quality is so important and it is so encompass-
ing that frequently God is referred to as a "God of love."

Prophets of various eras have emphasized that
charity, or this pure love of Christ, is so important that if
we do not acquire it through our life's experience, we have
nothing. There simply are no substitutes.

The greatest of all commandments deal with love.
This is consistent with the truth that love is the most important attribute. The greatest commandments deal with
love for God, self, and others. All other commandments
follow from these.

Those who are true disciples of Christ are identified
by their love. Such followers of Christ are diligently engaged in developing their love so that they may love others
in the same way the Savior loves them.

Misconceptions About Love Are Diverting

Unfortunately, the word *love* is used today in many
different ways. For this reason the word does not proffer a
clear understanding. Before attempting to make clear the
meaning of this pure kind of love, it is important to reject
outright some of the misconceptions which the word
invites.

For instance, pure love is not synonymous with a
sexual act. Many human beings have come to define love
in this very narrow way, but it is not the meaning which
the scriptures give. The sexual act is the culmination of the
sexual drives which both men and women have. These
strong feelings encourage men and women to set up their
own family units. Blessed by the marriage covenant and

sanctified by the commitment a man and woman make to each other as they establish a new family unit, these drives become a bond, satisfying and nurturing.

But if sexual drives are allowed to demand gratification without responsibility, the result is one of selfish, consuming, undirected passions which leave emptiness and often destruction of the soul.

There are many unrighteous actions born of the intensity of feeling aroused by the passions of sexual desire. These range from lust, adultery, and incest to self-stimulation and unnatural homosexual liaisons. These actions can never lead to the pure, life-giving, life-renewing love of Christ. In fact, because they have greater alliance to selfishness and unrighteous power over another, these actions lead one away from the joy-producing love which the word of God commends to mankind.

Pure love is not synonymous with emotion. Many associate the word *love* with an emotional feeling of acceptance. In the extreme this thinking leads one to believe that the depth of one's love is directly related to the intensity of the positive emotional appeal of something or someone. Godly love is not restricted in this way. We may feel a great attachment and appreciation for a person who fulfills our perceived needs. However, this too can be more selfishness than love. Someone may be fulfilling an immediate need at the expense of a more important long-range need, and our emotions alone would not allow us to perceive the difference. Healthy emotional feelings in relationships are good, but still may not be an indication of charity or pure love. There is a deep emotion in pure love but it is not an unrestrained, undirected response. People do not "fall" into pure love, they must climb up to it.

Charity is not indulging another. Frequently we are tempted to equate someone's love with their willingness to do as we desire. This is a gross misconception. Love requires that something be done when it is consistent with true principles, not when someone desires it. Often people ask others to do wrong things for selfish reasons. Sometimes we are inclined to say that if God loved us, He would protect us from the challenges and difficulties of mortal life. This simply is not so. The challenges are a part of the design. Our task is to develop strength of soul as we learn how to deal with challenges by being wise and responding to the needs of others even in the most difficult times. To remove challenges from our lives or to do for us what we must do for ourselves in order to progress would be to deprive us of the very purpose of mortal existence.

What Charity Is

Charity is a complete love. The pure love of Christ includes emotions, but involves much more. To love as Christ loves we must love with our entire souls. He taught clearly that we must love with all our hearts, with all our souls, and with all our minds. A love of this kind requires that we feel deeply, but that our emotions be perfectly controlled. It requires that we involve our mind, being perfectly influenced by true principles. To love perfectly we must know truth perfectly.

Charity is "other" oriented. Pure love is motivated by the needs of others. It leads us to respond to others' needs by serving them and even sacrificing for them. Our love is expressed in our deeds.

Charity is a love for everyone. We are required to love even those who abuse us. The greater challenge is met and the higher love exhibited when we love our enemies. Jesus Christ made it clear that such love was required, and provided an example of true charity when He asked the Father to forgive those who were crucifying Him. It is abundantly clear that love of this kind does not require that we approve the acts of all people. The actions of people can be despicable, and yet the love we have for the very same people can be perfect.

Charity is a love that endures through time. A pure love does not change with events. It is unfeigned no matter what circumstances exist.

Charity is an evidence of strength. When we have come to the point at which we know greater truth and make choices that benefit others, we are vastly stronger. Uncontrolled emotion is weakness. It makes one totally vulnerable to temptation and prevents coherent, helpful actions. Love is a source of peaceful power and binds us to other people more securely than can be done in any other way. Love motivates a desired response of warmth and of help.

To love as God loves, we must understand the needs of others, understand the true principles that apply in the situation, understand the priority of both the needs of those involved and the truths that apply, and then act, think, and feel in such a way as to provide maximum opportunity for others to improve themselves as a result of what is done. This kind of love is "other-oriented" and is the opposite of selfishness. We should strive to become other-oriented and to understand enough of need and truth to act for others in ways that will bless their lives.

None of us has a perfect understanding of all true principles, and none of us has the capacity to express perfect love for others. Therefore, even when we give our best effort, our acts and feelings are not always consistent with what Jesus Christ would feel and do in a similar situation. However, if our intent is charitable and if our acts are consistent with the best we know, we are succeeding. Christ has provided us with a guideline to help us test ourselves as we develop. He has taught that we will be doing the best we know how to do if we treat others as we believe they should treat us. This analysis requires that we evaluate our response to a situation against our best understanding of true principles.

What Grace Is

It is of great importance to understand that acts of grace are born of love. Love manifests itself in actions that influence the welfare of others. Grace is exhibited by one of greater stature acting for the benefit of another as a condition of the other's being favored. As we perform acts of love, doing for others what they cannot do for themselves, we perform limited acts of grace in their behalf. Jesus Christ and our Eternal Father, who understand our needs perfectly and who also understand all that is true, have provided for us through their grace opportunities that we could not develop for ourselves.

Charity Is the Source of Joy

Joy is experienced when we extend pure love. Joy endures forever. There is great fulfillment associated with learning true principles. This fulfillment is exceeded when these principles are used in loving acts of service for others. Being greatly concerned about and understanding the deepest needs of others and having the capacity to provide them opportunity to be better than they are make possible the most enduring joy of which we are capable. As already described, when we deeply care for the well-being and needs of others, we are subject to sorrow. Joy and sorrow are inseparable companions. Both are the result of pure love for others. When those we deeply love respond to opportunity in a positive way, we experience joy. When those we deeply love choose otherwise and separate themselves from us and our Eternal Father in Heaven, we experience our deepest sorrow.

Examples of Charitable Love

The following examples will help clarify the meaning of charity, or godly love.

Consider two mothers who have recently brought

children into the world. Each may have a deep emotional feeling for the little one she has nurtured. If one of them knows many true principles, including the ultimate potential of her child, she will be able to love the child far more deeply. Knowing the nature of the child and his relationship to God, the mother can understand his needs in different priority. She can act and think and feel in behalf of the child in ways that will give far greater opportunity and higher expectations than the other mother is capable of, no matter how sincere she might be. Knowing more of truth makes it possible for a mother to love more completely.

Men and women at all times and places have had and do have deep, personal needs. They have emotional and sexual capacities that are good and beautiful. They desire to be close to another and to share feelings, ideas, and experiences. These needs are also good and beautiful. Most men and women desire to have other souls need them, and they want to share with them these feelings and experiences. They desire to understand more of life and to have some pattern to follow and some reason for being.

The Savior, because of His love, has given us commandments to guide us as we try to fulfill these needs. He has told us that we must be love-oriented, not selfish. He has instructed us that intimate sexual relationships outside the bond of marriage are wrong. Not only are specific acts wrong, but simulation of the acts, substitute expressions, or even lustful thoughts concerning such acts are wrong. He has instructed us to control and direct our emotional passion (not to eliminate it) so that it might work toward our good and not destroy us.

The man or woman who understands the needs of his or her companion and who also understands the truth brings an eternal dimension to the relationship—a dimension which involves both partners in a profound and beautiful way. Outside the bonds of marriage there is little purpose or responsibility associated with acts of sexual intimacy. Inevitably there is an element of selfishness or gratification that motivates what occurs. In the process of participating in acts that involve the most sensitive part of one's being, where selfishness is the motivator, the soul is marred. The tender, beautiful capabilities become calloused, and feelings of abuse and ugliness develop. The needs of both the man and the woman persist over time, and acts of great intimacy that do not have long-term commitment and purpose are unfulfilling and are finally seen in their true form — selfish acts motivated by the desire for gratification.

It is possible for the man and woman who assume the responsibility of marriage to participate in intimate relationships in such a way that there is both purpose and responsibility in their experience. It is possible for them, by adhering to commandments or instructions consistent with eternal law, to be more deeply concerned for the greater needs and feelings of their companion than for their own. If they act consistent with the commandments that govern intimate relationships, they are able to develop and then participate in a oneness that is sacred and beautiful. They can participate in a relationship in which their most tender feelings and needs are shared completely. Furthermore, their experience will sometimes be the beginning of a process that will prepare a tiny, physical body for another of the spirit children of God, who is looking forward to an opportunity in mortality.

Our loving Father and the Savior are not depriving us by commanding us to restrict and control these activities. They want us to experience the complete beauty, tenderness, and freedom of a loving relationship with a companion. They want to protect us from the abuse of these capacities that would prohibit us from such beautiful experiences. Those who abuse themselves and others selfishly are not free to have the kind of relationship that those who live in harmony with true principles can experience. Self-stimulation, homosexual relationships, and all other substitutes are largely motivated by the desire for gratification without full responsibilities. Selfishness will never be a substitute for love. Knowing the deeper needs of the other, we would deny them, out of love, rather than yield to their request to indulge them.

There are many whose emotional and social development is not yet sufficient to allow them to meet the responsibilities of marriage. Nevertheless, it is wrong to assume that a substitute will ever provide the same kind of opportunity for growth and joy that the God-ordained marriage relationship can provide. Such individuals should work very hard to prepare themselves for the greater opportunity of which they will eventually be capable.

Those who may assume that because they are married they have license to be selfish are equally wrong. It is, of course, possible to be selfish within a marriage. This, too, violates truth. To know true joy, both the husband and the wife must love the other. Both husband and wife must apply true principles and act, feel, and think in ways that provide opportunities for the other. In such special relationships there is a joy, power, and freedom unknown to those who are selfish. The most enduring happiness that we know in life is the kind that develops in appropriate loving relationships with others. As you consider the most joyful people you know, it will be apparent that they are people who have developed a great deal of charitable love for others.

Chapter Eight

‖ The Personal Perfecting Process

In the search for truth it becomes increasingly clear that there are principles that govern the development of the soul. They are the same principles which govern the search for truth. However, in the perfecting process the emphasis shifts from seeking the intellectual, conceptual under-standing to applying the principle of continued self-correction or repentance and to charity or the application of truth in providing opportunities for others. In other words, the process shifts to being able to practice in daily circumstances the qualities of Christlike behavior. As we perfect ourselves by appropriately governing our daily lives by true principles, we gain a new capacity to under-stand and to love. This greater truth and greater love bring us closer to our Eternal Father and to Jesus Christ. We become one with them as this process continues and as we perfect our souls.

To know and properly to apply these principles makes success in pursuing the purpose of life possible. We are not promised that by applying these principles we will be shielded from problems, challenges, or tragedies. We are not promised that by properly applying these prin-ciples we will always acquire or achieve what we want. We are promised that these principles will lead us through problems, challenges, and tragedies to a more perfect soul. In order to make progress we must understand that this is the goal of perfection.

It is important to realize that since the work of perfecting the soul is an eternal process, individuals will be engaged in using all the principles simultaneously. These principles are discussed separately to facilitate understanding.

The single most important attribute of a godly being is pure love or charity. To have this kind of perfect love requires that we know all truth in proper perspective. Wisdom (truth in perspective) is a prerequisite for love. Therefore, wisdom is the second most significant attribute of God. Wisdom can come only after one has gained knowledge of true principles. All other godly attributes, such as patience, compassion, and justice, follow from wisdom and love. Our eventual goal, then, is to come to know all true principles in priority and to apply such principles in perfect love to every person in every condition. This is an incredibly demanding and optimistic task. Achieving even limited success results in peace and joy and continued opportunity. Knowing that this greater goal is possible for everyone encourages us to go on. Each step justifies the next. Given time and continued effort, the goal can be achieved.

Whatever our condition here in mortality, it can be improved. When we search for and attain some true principles and then alter the way we think and act so that we are, in fact, more loving, we have made progress. There is no limit to this process short of perfection. Until then we can always learn more and love more deeply. The total plan will provide everyone with a fair opportunity to pursue this process to its noble end. When our circumstances here in mortality provide us with greater opportunity, then we will be expected to make greater progress. When we know what the true purpose of life is, then we will be accountable for that knowledge and expected to assume the responsibility that inevitably comes with knowing such a truth. When our circumstances deny us the opportunity of knowing truth and the purpose of life, we are not accountable for what we do not know. Furthermore, we are promised that the opportunity will be provided later.

We Can Engage the Perfecting Process

The eternal principles that govern progress are:

Faith. We must believe in the possibilities to learn to love others, and to overcome problems and challenges. This belief in possibility must be coupled with hard work. Appropriate work activities range from prayer to laboratory experiments, but all require extended effort.

Revelation. The recognition of truth can come through a variety of experiences ranging from a quiet feeling of peace to a vision. The source of truth is the same in all revelations, including inspiration of loving action.

Repentance. As we understand truth, we can change in the way we think, act, and feel. Our lives can conform to truth and we can use the freedom and power of truth to serve others.

Enduring. We continue the process throughout mortal life and beyond. Perfection is a goal not reached in this world.

Faith, the First Principle

As in the process for discovering truth, the first step in perfecting the soul is to have faith sufficient to move one to action. The individual must believe that it is possible to perfect the soul. The knowledge of the truth clearly articulated by revelation is that men and women are the children of God with the potential of achieving perfection. Revelation also gives us a plain understanding that the perfection spoken of is the development of the divine characteristics of wisdom and charity, or the pure love of Christ.

Faith begins with the first whisper of hope and

grows as the individual accepts the hope and begins to live as though the hope were true. Faith in the Lord Jesus Christ is the first principle in the law of the gospel. For faith to exist or to develop in our souls there must be an awareness of or belief in the possibility of something. Faith develops, for example, when we begin seriously to consider the possibility that truth does exist and that it is knowable. Faith develops when we consider seriously the possibility that there is a personal God who knows and cares for each one of us. Faith develops as we seriously consider the possibility that Jesus Christ is exactly who He says He is—the Son of God, the Savior of the world, the Creator—and the one who has made it possible for us to accomplish the purpose of mortal life. Faith develops as we seriously consider the possibility that we are all children of God and brothers and sisters of Jesus Christ.

As we accept these truths the divine light of the possibility of eternal progression begins to guide our actions.

As soon as the possibility is accepted, the individual may begin the refinement of the soul. Preliminary to all actions is achieving an understanding of what kinds of behavior are most like the example of Jesus Christ. This requires a continuing, ongoing study of the word of God. It requires a never-ending study of the true principles which govern the world in order to "subdue" the earth or come to know and understand it.

Once the light is accepted and is allowed to enter the human soul by acceptance, it can begin to work. By conscious choice the individual begins to improve performance, especially as it regards gaining light and knowledge and as it is manifest in charitable acts.

It is not enough to believe in possibility. Assuming something is possible, we must next act on it. We must test it. We must implement it in our lives and evaluate the effect. We must study, ponder, search, and strive to extend our understanding of what is possible and what may be true. This is equally true in the intellectual struggle to articulate true principles, and in the application of those principles to personal behavior.

Different questions may require different forms of inquiry and different kinds of work, just as differing circumstances and personalities will require differing responses. Prayer is always helpful. It encourages a teachableness in us and a recognition that we need divine help in our progress.

After carefully considering the alternatives, we need to select the behavioral response which will be the most honest expression of love and concern for those with whom we associate. We must be mindful of the effect our lives have upon those with whom we share time and space and mutual concerns. We need to seek God's help in being sensitive to human need. When we ask, we need to listen and to respond to the promptings of the Spirit.

As we do kindly deeds, we will have greater and greater insight into the value of each response. Often a human problem will require more than one response. We need to implement all the good ideas that come to us and we need to remember that God urged each of us to express our love for Him by caring for the people with need among us.

We must always remember that in mortality our work will never be over. Once we have learned to do good to those we love and to those who love us, then we should try to do as Jesus Christ taught and do good to our enemies and to those who despitefully use us. Our progress toward personal perfection is very much like our search for knowledge of things as they are, as they were, and as they are to be. We find that each discovery leads to another and then another.

In the progress toward more Christlike behavior, as we practice the teachings of Christ we gain not only more ability to give love and caring, but also the individuals performing the loving service grow both in mind and in heart.

In fact there are some things that can be learned only from the experiences of living. One of these is the genuine enlargement of the heart as one goes about finding opportunities to give loving service.

In order for an athlete significantly to improve his skills he must believe that it is possible to do better. He must then engage a rigorous training and practice program. For a scientist to come to a still greater understanding of some part of nature he must believe that there is an underlying order to the events that occur. He must then pursue the laborious process of searching, studying, testing, and pondering. He must be open to previously unexpected results. To come to a greater ability to love others an individual must believe that he or she can love and can express that love; the individual also must believe that others' needs are important enough to be met. The struggle is to find a way to help others meet those needs in an appropriate way.

We must spend considerable time thoughtfully evaluating and consciously asking for understanding on how to help others meet needs. Intervals of prayer and pondering are essential. Fasting sometimes heightens our sensitivity to inspiration in this regard.

The athlete will not improve without stretching himself to the limit in his effort to do better. The scientist will never know greater truth if he refuses to test his hypothesis with experiments. The searching soul will never know God without testing the possibility of his existence by following the laws that lead to confirmation of this fact. The individual will never learn to love nor to become compassionate until he or she performs loving acts to another soul in need. To stop short of this would make it impossible to know more about God or to perfect one's own soul.

Revelation, the Second Principle

We have already considered the wide range of revelatory experiences. These experiences occur when we prepare for and then discern greater truth with the help of the Holy Ghost. In addition, revelatory experiences can direct us in the use of truth for the benefit of others. The Spirit can and will guide us to an understanding of how true principles can be used to fulfill the needs of others in expressions of charitable love. Our Eternal Father and His Son often influence our brothers and sisters through us. When we are prepared and willing, we receive divine influence to guide our efforts to provide opportunities for others. To seek for a clear understanding of what to do either to overcome a personal weakness or to aid another is an appropriate request for personal inspiration or revelation, because we know that the thought or the concept precedes the action.

Repentance, the Third Principle

Repentance is a self-directed change toward truth. For repentance to occur there must be an understanding of greater truth and a desire to change our thoughts, feelings, and actions until they are harmonious with this greater truth. Repentance is not accomplished until our lives have changed and the things we do are compatible with the truth we know.

Repentance is not restricted to changes in behavior alone. It is even more fundamentally related to changes in the way we think and feel. Changes in behavior follow. When our thoughts are consistent with truth, changes in behavior are more likely made for the right reasons and they are more likely to persist.

Repentance is required for all righteous change. It is obvious to many that taking from another against that person's knowledge or will violates eternal law. Those who do this must change in order to succeed in the purpose of life. It is less obvious that those who have the wrong belief about God need also to change if they are to fully succeed in the purpose of life. The nature of God does not depend upon our preference nor our agreements. If we have come to a view about God that is inconsistent with truth, then we are limited. Although we may do much good, we could do even more good and be even more successful if we changed our thinking about God to be more consistent with truth.

Change is also required when we acquire new understanding about the creations of God. For example, if a satellite makes new observations in space, we may be required to change our way of thinking about the solar wind, or about a planet or about a moon orbiting a planet. All changes we make that bring us into closer harmony with true principles bring us a better view of the world.

We sin when we refuse to repent and live in harmony with known truth. When, individually, we come to a knowledge of a true principle or commandment, then we no longer have the option of ignoring without consequence that principle in our lives. After learning a true principle we must change our lives to be consistent with it. When greater truth is revealed, greater responsibilities are acquired. We then either change to be in harmony with the truth or we consciously violate the truth.

It is important to understand the difference between error and sin. Both block the pathway to eternal progress, but they are not identical problems.

We entered mortal life as unknowing infants separated from God. As infants we were self-oriented and unable to respond to the needs of others. Thus we made many errors.

Both wisdom and love—the ultimate characteristics—are achieved only by conscious, thoughtful choice of thought and action. As we grow and develop from our infant state to mature adults we find the constant challenge to be whether we will choose to remain self-oriented or progress to a larger, other-oriented view. Wisdom and love can be experienced only by the choice to love others and to serve them.

As we develop wisdom and love in our souls, we experience a great peace and joy in spite of the tribulations and difficulties of life. Joy comes to those who learn and love.

The process of such learning probably will include many errors. The self-correcting process is triggered as we gain more knowledge and insight and strive to bring our actions into harmony with what we come to know.

Sin, on the other hand, is conscious choice to do that which we know to be a violation of the true principles we understand. This leads a person far away from the harmony of truth and the peace of the perfecting process. Continued choices of this kind increase the misery one experiences.

The correction required includes remorse for the sinful act, restitution for the aggrieved, and resolution to resume the search for the better way.

True repentance is dynamic. Like faith, repentance compels us to action. As we become aware of even partial truth we can consciously choose to redirect ourselves into a path consistent with what we have learned. We then commit ourselves to this new course that will eliminate any discrepancy between the truth we know and the way we live.

There are two ways that we tend to deal with these discrepancies. We are uncomfortable when we know our actions and thoughts are inconsistent with what we understand to be true. So we either repent or we harden our hearts until we are insensitive to the Spirit that helps us discern truth.

In order to successfully repent we need to desire truth more than anything else, and we must then desire to live in harmony with the truth we understand. Change is difficult. Repentance often requires that we give up habits, thoughts, and even possessions. Knowing truth, we are required to make choices. We will choose good (truth) no matter what it requires, or evil (sin) and its consequences. The choice for truth brings us into greater light and closer to God. The atonement of Christ works in our lives. The choice for sin separates us from God, and we fall into greater darkness.

The choice for truth eliminates inconsistencies in our lives. We develop integrity, and as we do, we become more and more one with God. The knowledge of truth and the realization that our lives are harmonious with the truth brings peace in the face of great difficulties and a joy that endures through time.

A contrite spirit is a prerequisite to repentance. It is needful to approach life amenable to change. Those who want to improve and who actually think about the benefit of incorporating new understanding into their lives are able to change.

A repentant person is a forgiving person. Bringing about righteous change requires that we forgive ourselves and others. We cannot progress unless we leave behind past errors. Accumulating mistakes by constantly bringing up in our minds things that should be left behind prevents us from experiencing full repentance. Our success and the success of our Eternal Father in Heaven as regards our progress to perfection requires that we leave past mistakes completely behind. We are also required to allow others to leave behind their errors as well. We must be forgiving of their actions if we want to bring about the full change of heart that will bring us closer to God.

A person who is repentant will be obedient to the commandments of God. When we come to understand a commandment and realize that it is an abbreviated statement of an eternal law, then we must be obedient to that enlightenment. Repentant persons change until they are obedient to commandments.

The evidence of true repentance is found in the way we live. Neither words nor tears are persuasive evidence of repentance. We are required to think, feel, and act differently. It is the way we live that makes clear to God and others the quality of our repentance. If we have truly changed and have become more like Christ as a result of our repentance, we will think thoughts that are more true. We will feel towards ourselves and others in a new way. We will behave more as Christ would behave in similar situations.

A fully repentant person recognizes that Christ has made it possible for us to forsake error and sin completely. Through the sacrifice of Jesus Christ it is possible to eradicate all negative effects of transgressing law. We must recognize His love for us in making possible this change. We must acknowledge that the opportunity for repentance comes from Christ's atonement.

Those who are unwilling to change or who cannot conceive of the possibility that they should change, cannot repent. When we allow ourselves to build walls of defensiveness, we prevent righteous change. Even if we have an understanding of the principle, if we refuse to apply it to the way we live, we remain separated from God. We are not required to accept anything but truth, but we must be willing to change in order to live lives consistent with the truth.

Repentance is one of the most hopeful aspects of knowing the truth. There is something divine in knowing that sins and errors can be left behind and a change made which is profound enough to provide a new life, unrestricted by ignorance and failure.

Enduring in the Process, the Fourth Principle

The process that leads to truth and to a more loving soul is a demanding one. The task of coming to a knowledge of all true principles and using that knowledge to provide opportunities for others in perfect love is demanding. It uncovers the nobility of man. Many engage the process and make significant progress, yet fail to endure or to continue in their efforts to learn more and progress even further. Some are tempted to be satisfied with just a single important event or interval during which things were learned and a step upward was accomplished. It would be so much easier if an event, or even a few events, would bring about the total transition required to reach the goal.

Only those who endure, which means they continue in the process of learning and loving more perfectly even beyond mortal life, can come to be one with God. There is no other way.

Children come into the world eager to learn, to develop, and to grow. Each child comes with a unique spirit developed in the premortal world. They come with different genetic traits imposed by their earthly parents. They also come into different environments that determine to a great extent what they learn. All children learn. They believe in the possibility of learning and at least at first eagerly work at learning. They are quick to learn and thus change as they respond to those about them and mimic those who teach them.

As we mature physically and assume a more adult role in life, we often end the process. We question the value of learning and often believe that the sacrifice required to learn is not justified.

Furthermore, we feel less need to learn. Others are now asking us questions. We become less pliable as we answer the questions. It is much easier to defend our preconceived judgments than to pursue the more difficult task of acquiring new understanding.

We must never lose our freshness and sense of wonder, even when we have come to understand some important things. Our acts and thoughts and their influence on others will be destructive if we do. As we observe these destructive effects we will be able to tell that we are not acting in harmony with truth. We should be more concerned about what we do and think and feel than about what we say. Our acts do convey what motivates us.

We are tempted to view those who seem to make great progress in life as somehow different than we are. We sometimes believe that they have never had to meet difficulties—at least not with the same severity that we have.

This is not true. All meet challenges. The challenges are not the same and do not occur in the same sequence, but all have challenges to overcome. The difference between those who succeed and those who do not is determined by the way they meet the challenges.

Those who become truly great acknowledge the problems or challenges. They put them into proper perspective by reminding themselves of other things that are also true. Then they proceed with great faith, believing they can do what is necessary to meet the challenge. They begin to work. They struggle, strive, explore, test, and try again. Their efforts bring insight and finally greater understanding. They apply additional truth and change the way they think and act. They may not always achieve their intended goal, but they do learn and become stronger. And that is the purpose of life.

As we succeed the challenges become greater. Understanding algebra may be all we can do early in life, but mastering algebra leads to the ability to learn and to apply the axioms and principles of calculus at a later time. The problems of youth are no longer as difficult for the more successful adult. The challenges of early adult years are frequently less demanding than those that come along later. There is no limit to our ability to learn, to improve, to develop, and to deal with challenges.

This increased expectation of growth is not only present for individuals but it is also established for groups of people. For people who have not progressed far, such as Israel in the wilderness, God may set His expectations in a series of commandments that deal with specific acts. He instructs the people to do this or not to do that. If they do as counseled by these commandments, they will live consistent with eternal truth.

When the people are reasonably able to live consistent with these expectations, they receive a higher approximation of eternal law. Jesus Christ added significant understanding when He taught that we should control even our thoughts and emotions. His great expectation requires extraordinary discipline and increased understanding.

Finally, as still greater truths are learned, it is possible for people to work together with increased creative capacity for good causes. They become more free and more powerful as a people, as well as individual children of God.

Our success is determined by our willingness to endure in applying the principles that govern growth. We do not have control over all things in life, but we do have control over the great personal, internal process of change that leads to personal perfection. The promise is not that life will be easy or that success will be given to us. On the contrary, the challenges will inevitably become more difficult as we progress. The promise is that by enduring or continuing the process, we will develop our souls until we accomplish the full purpose of life. We will learn more and more of true principles. As we learn we will be more and more capable of loving others and providing them with needed opportunities.

Mastering the capability of giving love as one endures trials and tribulations brings a quality of life unknown otherwise.

An Example of the Process Being Applied

My mother, Arta Romney Ballif, described an event that occurred during her mission to New Zealand. It clearly illustrates in a human life the process that we have been discussing.

The Samoan Brother

The meeting had been long, and the weary missionaries looked at the clock anticipating dismissal. The stillness was exceedingly still in the dimming twilight of the musty chapel as the Samoan brother arose to speak. He was short and plump, and his sad eyes filled with tears as he talked. He looked at the floor. He formed his words with care. "I sorry I not speak English," he said. "But I belief the Gospel true." His hands clenched the back of the bench in front of him. "I come to Auckland from Samoa so children go to school. Also, I belief the Gospel true."

The Samoan brother took his handkerchief from his pocket and wiped his perspiring forehead. He shifted his weight from his left foot to his right foot. He spoke softly but with feeling. "My wife come from Samoa with girl who is sick in hospital. My wife promise sick girl we come see now. I belief we should see her. President, he make me missionary. He call meeting. I belief the Gospel true. I belief we should do what Gospel say. I belief I should go with wife to visit sick girl. I belief I should come to meeting. I cannot do both at same time. I in trouble. I not know which should I should, I be excuse, please?

"I want to tell you one thing first," he said. He hesitated, searching for the English words that would best express his emotions. "I want to tell you one thing.

"I come home from work one day, and I come up steps of place where I lif, and I see dead cat on porch by door of my neighbor's house, man who lifs next to my house. Very close next. The cat was black and white, and it was dead already by door of his house. I see it. I go in my door. I shut door.

"Next day, I come home and I see dead cat on my porch next to my door. Dead cat, it is black and white, and it stink is not good. I go in house and shut door quick. I shut stink that belong to dead cat and cat hisself out. I say to children, 'Who put cat on our porch?'

"They say, 'Man who lifs neighbor to us. He brought it over and put it on our porch by door.'

"I was mad. I think to do neighbor mad. I say to children, 'Take dead cat. Put it back on his place, next to his door. Quick,' I say. I did not like dead cat. I did not like it stink. I did not like man who put it there. I think bad things of him.

"Children come back and say, 'We put dead cat on porch by door of man who lifs next to our place. We put it by his door. It smells bad.'

"Then I go out back of my place and I sit in chair and I think. And I full of big mad. I expect man next to our house to come out and say something. I expect he is mad, too. With two mads, that is too much mad. I wait. I think of stink of dead black and white cat."

The Samoan brother paused, heaved a great sigh, sniffed, and then continued. "After some little while, I think of who I am. And I belief the Gospel true. I think of Gospel. I think for long minutes. I go soft, and I hurt inside. I have confusion. Then I make decision. I say to children, 'Go get dead cat. Bring it over here. We bury it.'

"They bring dead cat. We bury it in back yard. We dig hole deep. We make box for dead cat. We put plenty dirt on top. After we finish putting dirt on top of stink, children say to me, 'We glad you bury dead cat. It is better thing to do. We like you for doing that.'

"Then I think of my children and the times I tell them Gospel true. I pleased with myself for showing children I belief Gospel true. I sit in chair and think. The mad is gone, gone somewheres. I not know where it is gone, but it is gone.

"Pretty soon, while I thinking and rocking back of my place, my neighbor come over fence. He look at me. I smiling some more. And he say, 'I did not like you Samoans living next to me. I not like it. I wish you stay in Samoa. I see you church people. I see you go to church every Sunday. I not know what church you go to, but now I glad you go to church. I see you belief your church. You lif right. I sorry I put dead cat on your house. I real sorry 'bout that.' "

The Samoan brother wiped his eyes with his handkerchief. He was visibly crying. "Brothers and Sisters, I belief we got to lif our actions. I belief the Gospel true. I not talk English. I sorry 'bout dead cat. I sorry 'bout language. That is all I got to say. Now I go to visit sick woman. You excuse, please? I sorry to leave, President, but you excuse? Lif your actions, so man who lifs next your house can see. Then he belief Gospel, too. I belief—You be happy . . .''

Overcome with emotion, he broke off, stood for a few moments, tears falling in big drops from his cheeks to the lapels of his smallish suit, then he walked apologetically, eyes and head drooping, along the aisle to the outer door. (Arta Romney Ballif, *The World and I* [Provo, Utah: Press Publishing Limited, 1977], pp. 82-83.)

It is clear from the beginning of the story that the Samoan brother and his wife were good people. They had come from Samoa to New Zealand with a sick child that they were attending to. When the neighbor put the dead cat on the Samoan's porch, he responded angrily and in a way that was inconsistent with principles he knew to be true. He sinned. He then applied the process.

First of all he renewed his faith by reminding himself that "the gospel" was true. He then contemplated the implications of his act in the light of gospel principles. As he pondered, it was revealed to him that he should correct his error and remove the cat from his neighbor's porch.

His children helped him carry out his act of repentance. In so doing he expressed charitable love for the neighbor who had "despitefully used" him. He felt peace and joy as he responded to the promptings of the Holy Ghost and brought his life into harmony with the principles of the gospel. His expression of love made it possible for his neighbor to progress as he was taught by example.

By enduring in this process the Samoan would become more and more like Christ and therefore succeed in the purpose of life.

Part Four

On Recognizing the Value of Divinely Given Organizations

Chapter Nine

|| The Family

The goal of life has to be pursued individually. No one can take from us the responsibility of the difficult task of perfecting our souls. We cannot assign the responsibility to another. We can all engage in the process that takes us through life's challenges in a way that will lead us to greater truth and love. We can come to know God and truth by personal initiatives. This I believe to be one of the most compelling of all the concepts revealed.

The purpose of life is precisely the same for everyone. All of us, black or white, bond or free, female or male, married or unmarried must strive to perfect our souls. There is only one gospel, one set of true principles, that applies to everyone.

The goal is the same for all of us, and yet the challenges we face differ enormously. Those who overcome greater challenges successfully make greater progress. Ultimately, everyone will have a full opportunity to succeed. The process should be engaged immediately.

It is not possible to succeed in our quest without significant interaction with others. We learn from others, and we also develop love for others as we live together.

In order to facilitate this work, God has instituted two divine organizations. They are the family and the Church.

The family is the most fundamental institution among us. It introduces us to our first great experience with partnership and provides the first effective arena for expressing compassionate love to others by giving us a small, compact unit of people tied together in bonds of a shared heritage.

> The family organization was instituted by God. All, who can, should assume the responsibility of a family.

> The purposes of the family are to bring children into the world, to provide the most effective laboratory to learn true principles and to discover how to apply them in charitable love, to fulfill needs in ways consistent with true principles, and to prepare for eternal relationships.

> Men, women, and children all have special challenges and opportunities within the family.

> Ignorance and selfishness are the most significant factors causing conflict and failure in the family. Success in the family is realized to the degree that true principles are learned and applied in charitable love.

The Family Has an Organization

The family organization was instituted by God. Adam and Eve were brought together to form the first mortal family. They were given each other to set the pattern in a family relationship. All of us have been instructed by God to follow this pattern. We are told to leave our parents and to cleave unto one another as husband and wife. We have been counseled to establish permanent family relationships whenever possible. The man should not be without the woman, and the woman should not be without the man. All of us need the opportunity provided in a good family, and whenever possible we are responsible to help build a strong family.

The family consists not only of a husband, a wife,

and their children, but also of grandparents and their parents. All generations are bound together in the family.

The Family Has Specific Purposes to Accomplish

One Purpose Is to Procreate

The parents in a family relationship participate with our Eternal Father in providing a mortal experience for His spirit children. The creative act of bringing a child into mortality is a sacred responsibility. The parents provide a body for the child. The spirit child of God enters the body and the mortal opportunity begins. Those who understand the purpose of life are particularly responsible to provide an opportunity for those spirit children who desire to come here. Parents who know true principles are best able to help children succeed.

A Second Purpose Is to Learn and to Love

The family provides the most effective laboratory experience for mankind. Family relationships provide the best of all opportunities for both children and parents to learn many fundamental truths and to develop the capacity to appropriately love others. The child is provided a situation where for many years the parents can influence, teach, direct, encourage, and teach again, all in an environment of great love. Children who are loved will learn by example and therefore be far better able to love others as they mature. Parents responsible for children and for developing their relationships with their spouses are constantly required to learn and then to apply what they learn in blessing and extending the opportunities of other members of their family. Even when the ideal family does not function completely it is the close family relationships that provide the best opportunities for individuals to develop this unselfish love. Knowing the ideal enlarges our vision of what is possible. The constant requirement to learn and then to give unselfishly to the others in the family accelerates the perfecting process for all who engage it.

It is important to understand that with each developing state in family relationships, we experience greater opportunity. As we succeed in early childhood under the loving guidance of parents, we become prepared for the more difficult challenges that come to us when we must relate to friends and classmates in school. Continued success prepares us for greater independence and greater responsibility. Success in the teen years prepares us for marriage and the still greater responsibilities of a new family. As we learn to love each other as a couple, children come and we are faced with the even more demanding responsibility of loving simultaneously several different children along with a spouse while all are changing. Finally, the children leave and begin their own family relationships. Then with an extended family, which is harder for us to influence, and with the continued responsibility to learn and to love, we face the most difficult time of mortality. This final interval in mortality is a time of great joy and great sorrow as we love so many more than we could in earlier years. Even with declining health we are required to extend ourselves to learn and to serve, to struggle upward toward that more perfect state.

A Third Purpose Is to Fulfill Needs

All of us have significant needs that can be completely fulfilled only in family relationships. There are minimum needs for mere survival that include food and shelter. Even these needs are most efficiently and effectively provided for in family relationships.

The deeper needs of all of us are the need to learn and the need to participate in loving relationships with others. Little children crave learning and with the slightest encouragement find great fulfillment in coming to understand things not known before. Families can provide an environment in which the desire to learn is reinforced until it becomes a way of life. Things learned need to be discussed with others. Husbands, wives, and children have frequent opportunity to fulfill their need to discuss important ideas and events with others. What is more significant, all of us struggle at some time to understand the meaning and purpose of life. We tend to search for something more significant than survival. The family is the very best place for this understanding to be acquired and discussed.

We have a desperate need to experience love. Tiny children often do not survive without love even if they have food and shelter. Our emotional and sexual needs can be appropriately fulfilled in loving family relationships in which true principles are practiced. In healthy families we can learn to discipline our needs so that they are harmonious with true principles. Emotional and sexual needs are then fulfilled in ways that help us develop and provide opportunities for others. The parents can fulfill each other's needs with understanding and love. Neither should take from the other. Both should give. Wise parents can help their children understand their needs and prepare to fulfill them in the right way and at the right time in order to live in harmony with truth. In this way no one is deprived, but the emotions are selectively controlled for the advantage of all. Security and purpose are provided as parents teach and live by true principles.

A Fourth Purpose Is to Prepare for Eternal Relationships

A fourth profound function of the family is to prepare members of the family for eternal relationships. Those who succeed in the purpose of life and develop godly attributes will be allowed to continue in family relationships in the celestial world to come. Only those who have developed in this way will qualify for that opportunity. For these people the Lord will fulfill his promise to provide continuing relationships for us in eternal family units. In that state we will share with each other and with our Father in Heaven in the creative acts yet to occur as the work of God goes on.

Partial Families Have Special Challenges

The optimum relationship in a family organization exists when there is a father and a mother who are both committed to the pursuit of relationships based on true principles and who are both striving to learn and to develop love for each other and the children they are blessed to bring into the world. However, for many reasons, there are a great many families with only one parent. The purpose of the family, even in these restricted relationships, does not change. The ultimate purpose is for all members of that family unit to progress. The family is intended to facilitate that growth. Single mothers or fathers are required to extend themselves to do as much as they can to provide the influence that both a mother and a father would provide. Many, sensing this greater responsibility, compensate enormously for their single parent situation. Grandparents, who are part of the extended family, are often able to expand their significant role and provide an even greater influence for good in the lives of the single parent and the children. The Church organization is intended to provide considerable help, and though it cannot fully compensate, the organization of the Church and the people in it provide a support to the parent. Individual neighbors also have the opportunity to provide assistance to help compensate for these limited family relationships.

Families with Mixed Faiths

In terms of the optimum relationship there is another circumstance which brings difficult problems. When parents do not share the same understanding of eternal principles and relationships there is stress and sometimes contention in the family. Families who find themselves in these circumstances will need persisting love and continuing effort to resolve differences and to arrive at an understanding of true principles.

When children do not share the faith and values of parents committed to true principles, there will be great sorrow and stress in the family. Again, it is understanding and living according to these principles that may allow eventual harmony to prevail.

Single Adults

Single adults without partners or children have very challenging circumstances to meet. They have the same ultimate goal, but they do not have the advantage of the family laboratory in which to learn and to serve. Wherever possible these individuals should work hard to prepare themselves for a marriage relationship. If marriage is not possible, then they should strive to have experiences that will approximate the experiences in a family in order to develop the attributes we all need to succeed in life. Living alone, without the continuing responsibility of a family, makes it very difficult to keep from developing a more selfish orientation toward life. If we are not constantly challenged to be concerned for the needs of others, it may be very difficult to develop understanding and love. It is far easier in these circumstances to pursue self-need, which is the opposite of love. Yet single people who choose to follow the teachings of Jesus and who choose to devote time, energy, and resources to giving loving service often become among the most noble in achieving progress in personal perfection.

Special Opportunities and Challenges for Women

Women, whether married or not, have the same

goal as men have. Individually they are charged to perfect their souls. They must each learn true principles and develop wisdom and love. As children of God they have all the capacity needed to reach this goal. They have no limitations.

Each woman is unique. She is born with talents and is under divine commandment to develop her talents. Each woman is urged to use her talents to bless others. There are unlimited opportunities for this service.

Through the Church and as neighbors to all, women have the responsibility to teach and to influence others through service. The quality of the community environment is no less a woman's responsibility than it is a man's. The only limitations are the individual woman's own understanding of what is true and her desire to serve.

Women are endowed with a special capacity to bear and to nurture children. With this great blessing and challenge comes tremendous responsibilities of great significance. The future of the human race depends upon a woman's unselfish decision to bring children into the world and to give them loving care through their tender, dependent years.

A woman who devotes her energies lovingly with great self-sacrifice to teaching her children the moral values of the gospel of Jesus Christ and who painstakingly trains them to accept their responsibilities and to give an excellent effort in all that they do—this woman is the first line of defense against all of society's most tragic social ills. At the same time she is the first line of offense in helping the children of God accomplish the purpose of life.

But the remarkable blessing, challenge, and responsibility of becoming a mother cannot circumscribe a woman's mortal existence or else she will not be able to fulfill her personal perfecting process and give the vision of eternal progress to her children.

Society needs the best each person has to offer if our

community environment is ever to reach harmony with the principles of truth. That means that each person must offer his or her best efforts and talents to the challenges of living together. Women too must contribute.

The Church requires the time and talents of women to carry out the work of teaching the gospel. Women serve as teachers and as heads and leaders of appropriate organizations. They are vital to the work of God on earth.

Another important challenge for all women is to develop healthy and appropriate partnerships with men. Neither men nor women can succeed in family relationships or in life if they are drawn into selfish competition. Unless there is cooperation, shared responsibility, and love, the ultimate purposes of life cannot be achieved.

God has made it clear that women, like men, are to be stewards over their time and talents while on earth. It is abundantly clear that women have to make thoughtful choices in order to accomplish the purpose of life.

Special Opportunities and Challenges for Men

The goal for men is the same as the goal for women. Men who are worthy are given special assignments by God. These assignments require an authority or priesthood. Men are responsible to serve as patriarchs in their families and as administrators in the Church. The authority they are given is continued only if they use it in a way that is compatible with eternal principles. If they abuse it in any way then this authority or priesthood is lost. It cannot be used selfishly or inappropriately to compel another man or woman. It can be used only in an attitude of love or service. When used appropriately this authority provides an efficiency and order in the Church and in families. The women share in these responsibilities with their husbands and other priesthood leaders. Where cooperation and shared responsibility is dominant, the arrangement is extremely effective. If the slightest selfishness develops, then both the authority and the effectiveness diminish.

There is a tendency in some men to abuse their authority. Having been given a little responsibility, they are tempted to extend it to areas where it does not apply or to an extent that is not appropriate. It is a great challenge for men to carry out their special assignments in a way that is consistent with true principles.

A second great challenge is that the man, like the woman, matures to the point where he must make increasingly difficult choices. There are multiple high priorities.

The man, like the woman, has the responsibility of making choices that will direct him toward the ultimate goal of life. He shares with his wife the responsibility of establishing a family and leading every member in it into an effective search for true principles and into a life of loving service. He also has responsibilities of great significance in helping the Church accomplish its purposes. Furthermore, whenever possible he is required to obtain the necessary resources for the family. All of these responsibilities are demanding and are never completed. Each day the man must make the difficult choice of how to use his time in order to meet all responsibilities appropriately.

The man must accept the responsibility of a family. He cannot assume that by marrying and, with his wife, by bringing children into the world that he has met his responsibility successfully. Even if he also provides the resources necessary to sustain the family, he is not yet succeeding. He must also be deeply involved in teaching and loving his children. He must devote his energies lovingly and with great self-sacrifice to teaching his children the principles of the gospel of Jesus Christ. He should be to his wife and to his children a superb example of someone who sees life as one grand learning experience, who teaches them how to learn, and who uses what he learns to bless them and others. The love he has for his wife and each of his children must be expressed warmly and unmistakably in all that he does.

The man also contributes to the lives of those outside the family. Much of this contribution will come in the work he does to sustain the family. He pursues that work vigorously and effectively. He teaches his children integrity, responsibility, and other values as they observe him use his talents in honorable work.

Sad to say, some men and some women are diverted from the purpose of life and pursue wealth and power for its own sake. They rationalize that they will do good with what they accumulate. Pursuing wealth leaves little time for pursuing truth. Striving for power crowds out the desire to be charitable.

Wealth and power are not intrinsically evil. In fact, they are often acquired by good, thoughtful people who work hard and cooperatively with others. The resources acquired and the influence that comes make it possible to accomplish great good. When the resources needed to sustain life have been secured, it is possible to use the excess to facilitate our search for truth and to provide similar opportunities for others. It is also possible to use positions of influence to serve others and to encourage them to pursue the purpose of life. It is when wealth and power are sought for as an end that they become an obstacle and stop our progress. Furthermore, those with wealth have the responsibility of seeking opportunities to be aware of the intense suffering of those without resources, and to find ways to use what they have to sustain others and to help them find opportunities to become self-sustaining.

Fortunately, many men become increasingly wise and turn their energy, talent, and resources toward others. They are noble men who lead their families and others to truth and love and joy.

Special Challenges and Opportunities for Children

The goal for children is, of course, the same as it is for women and men. It is simply more distant.

Children born into a good family have the great blessing of an extended interval of learning before they have full responsibility. Unlike other living things, they have the capacity to make moral choices, and they have many years to experience the love and direction of parents who should provide for their needs and who should teach what is true by word and deed.

Young children have much to learn, and they believe without question that they can learn and change. In this state they pursue the perfecting process naturally. They are still free from the scars of fear, pride, and sin that harden the heart and prevent righteous growth.

Not only do parents have a responsibility to their children, but children have a responsibility to their parents. Choices made by children can be wrong even when the parents have provided very fine opportunities. It is not true that all the wrong choices and problems of children are the fault of parents. Children must assume responsibility for their choices even when they are quite young. They must begin the perfecting process, take advantage of whatever truth is available, and develop concern for others' feelings.

The Source of Conflict and Failure in the Family Can Be Identified

Ultimately, ignorance and selfishness are the sources of conflict and problems in relationships. When members of families do not understand the needs of others or the truths that apply, they are incapable of loving them. If members of a family are unwilling to let the needs of others in the family be more important than their own needs, they cannot strengthen the family relationships.

The problems will always carry labels of "financial difficulties," "incompatibility," and similar descriptions, but underlying all these is ignorance and selfishness, at least on the part of one of the partners. Where marriage fails, there is too little truth, too little love, and too little commitment. Truth and love bring success in families and in life.

Chapter Ten

The Church of Jesus Christ of Latter-day Saints

It seems to me the great value of the Church organization is that it gives opportunity and support to the individual in his or her personal efforts to develop and apply wisdom and love in daily living. The Church is named after Jesus Christ who implemented the great plan of our Father and who made it possible for us to accomplish the purpose of life. The title of the Church also includes a reference to these latter days to acknowledge the reestablishment of the same church organization that existed in earlier times to offer strength and encouragement to those disciples of Jesus Christ who lived at that period. Though many refer to the Church as the "Mormon Church," that is only a nickname taken from a great prophet of the Book of Mormon. The correct name is The Church of Jesus Christ of Latter-day Saints.

The Purpose of the Church

The purpose of the Church, as described by the prophet Spencer W. Kimball, is threefold:

- To proclaim the gospel of the Lord Jesus Christ to every nation, kindred, tongue, and people;
- To perfect the Saints by preparing them to receive the ordinances of the gospel and by instruction and discipline to gain exaltation;

- To redeem the dead by performing vicarious ordinances of the gospel for those who have lived on the earth.

All three are part of one work—to assist our Father in Heaven and His Son, Jesus Christ, in Their grand and glorious mission "to bring to pass the immortality and eternal life of man." (Moses 1:39.) (*Ensign*, May 1981, p. 5.)

When the central part of the gospel of Jesus Christ was again restored and it was known that we are all the children of God with the capacity to become like Him, then the purpose of the Church could be understood. The Church exists to assist in the process of perfecting souls. Whatever the current state of the sons or daughters of God, the Church provides opportunities for all individuals to learn and to apply true principles. They can all begin where they are and pursue the process that leads to eternal life. "Every soul is capable of enlargement," the Prophet Joseph Smith revealed to us, and if we begin the process and pursue it long enough, we can and will succeed in the purpose of life. The Church is concerned about every individual. It provides assistance and opportunity to families, to partial families, and to individuals. It provides assistance to the weak and to the strong. It teaches a doctrine of improvement for all.

It will become evident to anyone who seriously investigates the Church and its structure that the organization and administration of the Church is designed to allow maximum member participation. The programs of the Church give abundant opportunity for members of all ages to learn and to voluntarily serve others.

The Organization of the Church

The Church is presided over by three quorums and a bishopric. These quorums are: the First Presidency, the

Quorum of the Twelve Apostles, and the First Quorum of the Seventy. In addition, there is a Presiding Bishopric. Those who serve in these callings are referred to as General Authorities of the Church. The demands of their callings in a rapidly expanding church require that they devote their full time and energy to this service. Therefore, when necessary, these few leaders are provided a living allowance in order to sustain their families. All other leaders of the Church are responsible to provide a livelihood for their families in addition to their service in the Church.

The leaders of the Church are called after thoughtful, prayerful evaluation by those in authority over them. Revelation from God is the most important element in the process. All leaders are sustained in their offices by vote of the membership of the Church.

The sustaining by members does not constitute an election but signifies that the members know of no reason why the leader should not perform the service required by the office, and indicates their willingness to give support. The members commit themselves to help the person succeed in the task he has been called to perform. Members are entitled to the confirming spirit as they consider sustaining those called to lead them.

The President of the Church, who has received all of the authority to administer the affairs of the Church, delegates authority to others to the degree needed in order for them to carry out their more limited responsibilities.

All leaders of the Church, except for members of the First Presidency, the Quorum of the Twelve, and part of the First Quorum of the Seventy, are called to positions with the understanding that they will serve in that assignment only for an interval. Later, others whom they once served will serve them. Some principles can be learned only by service and thus the opportunity needs to be shared by all. For this reason the Church organization has been provided to give continuous opportunities for service.

Members find themselves simultaneously serving and being served much of the time.

A more detailed outline of the organization of the Church and the officers of the Church appears in the appendix.

Priesthood

The authority to act for God on earth is given by God to men as "priesthood." Men and women who are called to assume responsibilities in the Church must receive their assignments from someone who has this authority.

Unfortunately, often the word *authority* connotes force and subjection of others to the one with authority. Even more unfortunately there is a tendency for some with authority to abuse it and to take advantage of others. It must be emphatically stated that the authority of priesthood cannot be abused in this way. It has been made clear that whenever anyone abuses priesthood authority by attempting to exert unrighteous influence over others, his priesthood is lost.

Priesthood assignments are given to provide extraordinary opportunities to serve others. They can be accomplished only with wisdom and love unfeigned. Priesthood authority empowers us to serve and to love others with the Spirit and power of God.

It is also of great importance to understand that all of the blessings available to men through their priesthood assignments are also available to women. Men called to priesthood leadership positions are called to serve both men and women. All of the benefits come to both.

A further discussion of the priesthood is found in the appendix.

Programs

In conjunction with the organization of the Church a number of fundamental programs are developed and carried out to help bring about the threefold purpose of Church organization outlined by President Spencer W. Kimball.

Among the most noteworthy of these programs are the following:

— A continuing education program designed to teach the membership the essential elements of the gospel and to encourage their continued effort to apply the principles in their daily living.

— An extensive missionary program staffed by dedicated volunteers and financed by contributions of the participants, their families, and others who support the work. (Members of the Church sacrifice considerable time and money in an attempt to give everyone in the world the opportunity to examine and learn the principles of the gospel that make it possible to accomplish the purpose of life.)

— A welfare program that teaches members to work to provide for themselves, to upgrade their employable skills, to store in times of plenty in order to take care of themselves in times of scarcity, and to give of surplus resources for the care of the sick and the needy.

— A genealogy program which encourages us to study our ancestry in order to provide for them vicarious ordinance work which allows people who have preceded us in death to accept the gospel in its fulness if they desire.

— A youth program which features many activities, cultural programs, and service projects.

A more detailed description of the programs is found in the appendix.

Church Finances

Members of the Church provide through a voluntary tithing of their income the resources needed to operate it and to basically finance the programs it provides. In addition, they fast one day a month and donate at least the equivalent cost of the food not eaten to provide for the poor. Additional resources come from special contributions.

The Mission of the Church Is Implemented in Many Ways

God has directed the organization of His church in order to help His children accomplish the purpose of mortality.

Revelation to the Church

Through the prophets who lead the Church, God reveals true principles and gives special instructions. The prophet communicates with God and directs the Church in the way he is instructed. Though a great deal of truth has already been revealed, there are still many great and important things yet to be revealed. A prophet is needed to receive this revelation for directing the Church and to teach it to all who will listen. God is vitally concerned with the people of today, and His ways of helping them continue unchanged. He reveals true principles through his prophets to provide instruction and opportunity for mankind. He testifies to us of the atoning work of Jesus Christ and assures us of our worth and our familial relationship to Him. The great advantage of a prophet does not remove the individual responsibility we have to seek personal revelation in our own quest to understand true principles.

The prophet's role is also important in maintaining the purity of the doctrine of the Church. It is his responsibility to clarify and to interpret the doctrines and the scriptures.

The record of God's church and the revelations given by God to His prophets are recorded in the scriptures. Constant study of the word of God revealed through His prophets is required if we are to know that which is true and thereby be able to serve and to love others. Keeping these words in our mind will help us act and think and feel more and more as Christ would in similar circumstances. This study helps us invite the verification of truth through the Holy Spirit promised in the scriptures and by the prophets of all times.

We accept the Bible as scripture and adhere to its teachings with great conviction. Nevertheless, we do acknowledge that in the many translations of the Bible some errors have crept in. We use the King James Version of the Bible as an accepted scripture.

We also accept the Book of Mormon as scripture. It is a divinely inspired record made by prophets of the ancient peoples who lived on the American continent. This book provides a brief record of the people and, more important, another testimony of the universal mission and message of Jesus Christ. He revealed His gospel to these people and established His church among them.

The Book of Mormon was translated by the Prophet Joseph Smith from a set of gold plates. The teachings of the prophets recorded in the Book of Mormon make it clear that the same truths taught in other times and in other places were also taught to the people in America. It is the same gospel. The record in the Book of Mormon clears up some of the apparent conflicts that exist in the Bible. The two books, joined together, become a powerful source of truth.

The Doctrine and Covenants and the Pearl of Great Price contain additional revelations that are part of our scriptures. These short books provide clarification of the gospel. From time to time additional revelations are added to the Holy Scriptures to provide the cumulative advantage of God's continued counsel to mankind. These additional doctrines are added to the Doctrine and Covenants.

Opportunities to Learn, Practice, and Teach the Truth

The work of the Lord through all time has required that the gospel be taught to the inhabitants of the earth. Ultimately everyone must hear the true principles of the gospel and have the opportunity to accept or reject it. The programs and activities of the Church are largely devoted to teaching the gospel both to those who are now members of the Church and to those who are not.

It is not sufficient to learn true principles. It is required that we use the truth we acquire in providing loving service for others. We must develop love as the central attribute of our soul. The Church provides great opportunity for us not only to learn true principles but also to apply them by serving others without any compensation except the joy that comes from loving other people. Therefore, in all of the previously described organizations of the Church we are asked to perform responsibilities in such a way that we bless others. At every age members of the Church are given opportunities and responsibilities to help others. Understanding the purpose of life justifies a church organization that is always dynamic, providing individuals with new and increasing opportunities for growth. The purpose is not to have programs that are precise and finished. The purpose is to have all members participate in such a way as to develop their talents, to learn, and to love others by serving them.

The Opportunity to Participate in Ordinances

God's people have always been a covenant people. He has made it clear that a very important part of His instruction is carried out through willing participation in covenants. By making covenants with God we are not only taught but we also are motivated to reach up to our greater potential as members of His family. The covenants we make are everlasting in nature. The covenants specify the conditions for blessings or opportunities that have eternal duration. God encourages us to think clearly about our responsibilities. He sets the bounds and conditions of eternal law in the covenants and makes it clear that if we live in harmony with those bounds and conditions, He will assure us of the opportunities and freedoms consistent with that law. When we violate the covenants, we have no promise. The required covenants for members of the Church are discussed in the appendix and include such things as baptism and confirmation.

All of the organizational work of the Church is designed to provide perfecting opportunities—opportunities which encourage members to learn and to love in the great spirit of charity described in the scriptures.

There are many vivid examples of the value of such organization-initiated experiences. One of the most remarkable occurred in Holland after the end of World War II.

The Church leadership in Salt Lake City had gathered together a large quantity of food and blankets and other such supplies from their storehouses and from the contributions of the people.

The prophet George Albert Smith asked President Harry S Truman of the United States for a ship in order to send the goods to the starving people in Europe.

After these goods had been divided among the peoples in Holland and other places in Europe, the principles of the welfare program were taught to the members of the Church in Europe.

The members of the Church in Holland were asked to grow potatoes and send their surplus to the starving members of the Church in Germany. This was a very difficult thing for these people to do. The Germans, at that time, were their enemies, and they were at first horrified at the idea of sending them potatoes.

But in deference to the word of the prophet they did send the food to the German people. The result, they testify, was that they learned to love and to discontinue their hate.

Afterword

What is the value of the synthesis presented in this book? To me there are compelling reasons why everyone should struggle to understand and carefully test the principles discussed.

First, these principles are important because they are true and because they govern our lives. Many important things are not yet known. Additional revelation will certainly come and enrich and expand what has already been made available to us. Nevertheless, what is known of truth is of great significance and cannot be ignored without serious consequences, including a limited, less joyful life.

The synthesis given is important because it provides appropriate perspectives and relationships. I found that developing this framework of principles allows me to evaluate all ideas and possibilities more effectively. It facilitates continued study.

I believe that understanding the nature of God, the nature of mankind, the relationship of God to man, and the divine potential of mankind gives us great motivation to learn and to love others. This understanding gives us great purpose that sustains us in the challenges and tragedies that inevitably occur. It motivates us to accomplish the work required to succeed in the purpose of life.

I believe the challenges of life are more easily met when we realize that there is only one approach to the pursuit of truth and the pursuit of improved behavior. All problems and all opportunities yield to this one set of eternal principles. These principles do not necessarily lead to wealth, power, and fame, but they always lead to greater wisdom and a greater capacity to love others. These principles, if followed, guarantee a peace and happiness that endures. They guarantee a more perfect soul.

These principles also lead to a quality of life characterized by a positive, forward-looking view and a life filled with warm, human, and more divine relationships with others. This more joyful life will be experienced whether one is poor or wealthy, male or female, black or white, bond or free.

Finally, these principles are significant because opportunities in this life and opportunities in the continuing life hereafter are available only to those who understand and follow them. Only those who develop the attributes of Jesus Christ will have opportunities to participate in the creative work that will go on in the life to come and will continue to enjoy family relationships.

Both the family and the Church can provide great help as we pursue the purpose of life. Through these divine organizations we can accelerate our search for wisdom and greatly increase our ability to love others. I am grateful for and indebted to the members of my family for their constant love and encouragement. I am also grateful for the Church that has given me great opportunity.

Only part of the conviction I have can be described in words. The exhilaration that comes from learning and the joy that comes from loving others can only be fully understood when it is experienced. This exhilaration and joy cannot be given; it must be earned. Fortunately it is accessible to everyone.

Appendix

The Organization and Ordinances of the Church

The Organization of the Church

The First Presidency

The First Presidency of the Church is the presiding quorum. It is headed by the President, who is the prophet of God on earth. Two counselors work with the President to make up the First Presidency. On occasion circumstances may require that an additional counselor or more be called to this quorum to allow the work to be carried out.

The Quorum of the Twelve Apostles

The Quorum of the Twelve Apostles consists of twelve men who are called by revelation through the prophet of God. These men are special witnesses of the Lord Jesus Christ. They proclaim His gospel and with the other quorums carry out the mission of the Church. This quorum is presided over by a president, who is the senior member of that quorum. The Apostles go to all the world bearing testimony of Jesus Christ and of the restored gospel, and, under the direction of the First Presidency, they organize and supervise the organizations and programs of the Church.

The First Quorum of the Seventy

The First Quorum of the Seventy is made up of special representatives who administer the programs of the Church around the world. They act under the supervision of the Quorum of the Twelve Apostles and the First Presidency to see that the doctrine and programs of the Church are being taught and carried out appropriately in each of the thousands of Church units around the world. The First Quorum of the Seventy has only as many members as the prophet believes are necessary. When the time comes that more than seventy are needed to carry out the work of the Church, a second quorum of seventy may be formed.

The Presiding Bishopric

A bishop and two counselors are called by revelation through the President of the Church to supervise the temporal affairs of the Church. Many important services are made available to the members of the Church through this bishopric.

General Officers of the Church

At the present time certain individuals are called to be general officers of the Church so that they may carry out particular assignments relating to programs which are administered by local leaders throughout the wards and stakes.

Among the most important of these are the following:

The general presidency of the Relief Society—these three women, a general president and her two counselors, head the organization for women eighteen years and older in the Church.

The general presidency of the Sunday School—these three men, a general president and his two counselors, head the organization that directs the study of the gospel by members of the Church in Sunday School classes.

The general presidency of the Young Men—these three men, a general president and his two counselors, lead the young men ages twelve to eighteen of the Church.

The general presidency of the Young Women—these three women, a general president and her two counselors, lead the young women ages twelve to eighteen of the Church.

The general presidency of the Primary—these three women, a general president and her two counselors, direct the program for the children of the Church.

The presidencies each have a board—each board differing in size—to work with them in furthering the work of the Lord through that organization.

Local Organization of the Church

The local organization of the Church, where it is fully functioning, is made up of *stakes* and *wards*. Where the Church is newly established and developing, the organization is divided into *districts, branches,* and even smaller units.

Stakes. A stake is a Church organization of approximately two to three thousand members. It is made up of several wards and sometimes branches and is presided over by a president, two counselors, and a high council consisting of twelve men. Three women preside over the womens' organizations of the stake, and many other stake officers provide leadership service as well. The president of the stake is called to that assignment by a General Authority of the Church. He and his counselors, the high council, and other stake leaders are sustained in their offices by members of the stake.

Wards. Stakes are composed of several wards. A few hundred members of the Church who live in a specified geographic area are brought together as members of the ward. The ward is presided over by a bishop and two counselors. The bishop is recommended by the stake president, approved by the general councils of the Church, and sustained by the members of the ward. The bishop acts under the supervision of the stake president to carry out the appropriate Church programs for the members of his ward. A president and two counselors are called in each ward to preside over the Relief Society. This organization provides all of the women in the ward with opportunities to learn and serve. Most members of the ward, including many of the very young, are called to carry out leadership and service assignments. From time to time through revelation these assignments are changed to give everyone opportunities to serve and to progress.

All members of the ward meet together weekly. This sacrament meeting is the most important meeting held in the Church at the ward level. At this meeting the members instruct one another and renew covenants made with God.

Priesthood

The authority to act for God on earth is given by God to men as "priesthood." Men and women who are called to assume responsibilities in the Church must receive their assignments from someone who has this authority.

The Aaronic Priesthood. This priesthood is a preparatory priesthood. It is named after Aaron, a valiant leader and spokesman for his brother, the prophet Moses. All worthy young men of the Church receive this priesthood when they are twelve years old. The Aaronic Priesthood is also given to those men who are older than twelve as soon as they are ready to assume the responsibility. New male members of age are given the Aaronic Priesthood.

Those holding the Aaronic Priesthood are given responsibilities that allow them to serve in the temporal affairs of the Church. They have regular assignments that require time and effort to fulfill. They are also assigned to aid in the teaching responsibilities of the Church. Through these opportunities for service the young men and new members of the Church prepare themselves for still greater responsibilities.

The Melchizedek Priesthood. This priesthood allows men to administer the spiritual affairs of the Church. It is named after the king of Salem, a great high priest. It is actually the Holy Priesthood after the Order of the Son of God. The name Melchizedek is used out of reverence to God and to avoid using His name too frequently.

This priesthood is given to those men who are worthy to lead in their families and in the organizations of the Church. It provides the right of service. It can never be used in pride or to fulfill men's vain ambition. Whenever an attempt is made to use it in this way, the priesthood or authority is lost. Though some may deceive themselves, they cannot act for God in unrighteousness.

The Relief Society

All women in the Church have the opportunity to participate in the Relief Society. The Prophet Joseph Smith stated that the organization of the Church was not complete until this women's society was organized and functioning.

The Relief Society is a vigorous organization that provides great opportunity for the women to learn and to serve. The women participate regularly in classes for important educational experiences. They also arrange and carry out service projects. They provide for those individuals and families who are ill and bereaved. They sponsor and participate in concerts, programs, socials, and a wide range of activities. Through these activities the women acquire greater understanding and conviction of true principles, their families are strengthened, they are motivated to encourage and support their husbands and sons in their responsibilities, and they develop and express charitable love through compassionate service.

Women in the leadership of the Relief Society sit in council with the men and contribute significantly in all of the affairs of the Church. Many thousands of women serve in teaching and leadership assignments in the Church.

Other Auxiliary Programs

There are programs in the Church that provide meaningful activities for members of all age groups. The programs are administered by the members and provide opportunities for them to learn from and to serve each other.

The Sunday School. Members of the ward who are twelve and older meet together each Sunday to study the gospel. In their classes the doctrines of the Church are studied. The texts used for study are the scriptures and manuals prepared to help the members understand the scriptures.

The Young Women Program. Between the ages of twelve and eighteen all women participate in the Young Women program. The central part of the program consists of class work and service projects. This program provides opportunities to develop through a wide range of activities and experiences. For example, the young women may participate in dramas, musical programs, athletic events, dances, and service projects. They study special interests and develop close relationships with each other and their adult supervisors. They have a goal-setting program which helps them direct their growth in many areas. To a large degree they plan and carry out their own programs with the advice and encouragement of women called to assist.

The Young Men Program. After age twelve and before age eighteen or nineteen, all single boys participate in the Young Men program. The significant core of this program involves class work and service projects. The early part of this program includes Scouting with all of its activities. The young men may participate in a variety of activities, including dramas, musical programs, athletic events, and service projects. Some activities are held jointly with the young women, although dating is not condoned until after the sixteenth birthday. Young men, like the young women, assume more and more responsibility for the programs as they get older. They are helped greatly by the men who advise and counsel them.

The Primary. Young children from the ages of one and a half to twelve participate in a Primary program. Teachers meet weekly with each age group, instruct them in the gospel, and help them understand how it should be applied in their developing world. The little ones sing, speak, and participate in activities that help them learn, and become better able to work with their young friends.

Other Programs

The Church develops other programs as needed and when justified by the circumstances at the time. Programs for young adults and older single members vary according to need. The following continuing programs are of special importance.

The Church Educational System. Because of the intrinsic requirement that all members have to learn and to grow, the Church provides educational opportunities for its members. All around the world young people meet together in early-morning *seminary* classes, or work through correspondence lessons to study the gospel and the history of the Church. College-age students continue the study in *institute* classes taught in buildings adjacent to many colleges and universities. The Church also provides fine educational opportunities at several higher institutions, including Ricks College, Brigham Young University, and BYU–Hawaii.

The Missionary Program. A central purpose of the Church is to provide everyone the option of hearing the gospel of Jesus Christ. Therefore, missionary activity is a responsibility shared by all members. The doctrine cannot be imposed on others. However, as members of the Church we have the conviction that the most important thing we possess is our understanding of eternal principles and that we have been charged by God to make these principles available to others. Therefore, we feel both a moral responsibility and a great desire to do what we can to share what we love most with others. Only then can others make choices with understanding.

The young people of the Church, both men and women, enthusiastically respond to the encouragement they receive to serve full-time missions. They interrupt their schooling or work and accept a call to serve wherever they are needed. About half learn a foreign language in order to serve in their missions. Most, usually with the help of their families and friends, pay for the cost of their mission themselves. In this work they go to the place of assignment and do their best to make friends, teach the doctrine they believe, and give others an opportunity to make informed choices.

Mature couples and older single women are also called to serve missions. They leave their grandchildren and homes and go wherever they are assigned in order to serve others. They use their savings, often supplemented by gifts from their children, to finance their missions.

Experienced leaders in the Church are called to supervise the missionary work. The president of a mission and his wife leave their vocation and home for a few years to direct the work of the missionaries in the area to which they are assigned.

Members of the Church sacrifice considerable time and money in an effort to give everyone in the world the opportunity to learn gospel principles and thus make it possible to accomplish the purpose of mortality.

The Welfare Program. Members of the Church believe in work. We are committed to a life of personal responsibility and to helping those who are not able to care for themselves. We believe in being prepared to take care of ourselves and our families. This requires vocational preparation, good management of resources available to our families, and a reserve of food and money.

In addition, wards and stakes often work together to produce food and goods that can be shared with those who are unable to care for themselves. People of all ages and vocations work together to grow food on farms, prepare food, and collect, repair, and distribute clothes and household articles to provide for those who need help.

The Genealogy Program. Because of our strong belief in families and in the possibility of continued family relationships beyond mortality, we study our ancestors. We search the records to learn all we can about those in our families who have preceded us in mortality. When the records are obtained, we perform vicarious ordinances for these people if the ordinances were not done in mortality. This makes it possible for those who have gone on to accept the work, if they now desire it. If they do not accept it, the work has no meaning.

We also prepare our own records for our posterity. All of us are encouraged to write a journal of important events and to summarize our convictions for the benefit of generations yet to come.

Church Finances

To operate the Church organization and to finance the programs described, it is necessary for the members to provide the required resources. This is done through the principle of tithing. According to this divine law, all members are to contribute 10 percent of their increase annually for this purpose.

In addition to tithing, members of the Church contribute a significant amount to provide for the poor and to maintain church buildings.

The Saving Ordinances

The fundamental ordinances of the Church are as follows.

Baptism

After someone has come to the point of believing in the possibility of striving toward an improved life and is open-hearted with a spirit amenable to change—and shows this by striving to keep the commandments—he is asked to make a covenant with God that he will truly follow after Him and strive to be like Him. The Savior Himself underwent this ordinance to illustrate its importance and how it was to be done. Someone having authority to function for God performs the ordinance, and at the conclusion of the baptismal pronouncement immerses the candidate in water. The individual comes forth with the promise that if he pursues his part of the covenant, all that he has done that is not consistent with what God would have him do will be forgotten. God promises that this symbolic rebirth will start the individual on the way toward a perfected life and the opportunity to be reunited with Him.

Confirmation

After baptism, someone with authority confirms newly baptized members of the Church and bestows on them the gift of the Holy Ghost. As members of the Church and as those having made commitments through the baptismal covenant, we are now given direct and continuing access to that Spirit which testifies of truth. This accelerates success in our efforts to learn and to improve. As participating members of the Church we share in the responsibility of accomplishing the work of the Church. We are blessed by the Church in our personal lives as we learn true principles, practice them, and teach them to others in acts of love. The Holy Spirit guides us as we pursue our work.

The Sacrament

The baptismal covenant is renewed frequently by members as they participate in the sacrament of the Lord's Supper. The covenant is renewed weekly when members of the Church eat bread and drink water in remembrance of the flesh and blood of Jesus Christ and renew their promise to follow after Him. The bread and water taken are symbolic of the flesh and blood of Jesus Christ. The sacrament provides a time of contemplation and renewed determination to keep within the bounds and conditions of the covenant we made at the time of baptism.

Melchizedek Priesthood

Male members of the Church who qualify accept the responsibility of the Melchizedek Priesthood in the form of a covenant. We renew our promises to keep God's commandments and to use the priesthood in accordance with the conditions set forth by God. He, in turn, promises us all the blessings that can come as a result of living in harmony with these truths.

Endowment

Some time after baptism, when members of the Church have made significant progress, we go to temples to participate in a more specific and a more binding covenant. In the temple we participate in a personal endowment. In this service we make a series of very specific promises. For example, we covenant to live the law of total chastity. We also covenant to do all we can to further God's work on earth. By keeping the greater law given, we qualify for greater peace and joy in this life and celestial opportunities hereafter. These covenants, made willingly, are embedded in a teaching presentation that outlines the preparation of the world and the purpose of life. The endowment is a more specific covenant than the baptismal covenant, but is in some ways essentially of the same nature. Like the baptismal covenant, it is a teaching device used to focus on specific commandments and to relate the bounds and conditions of the true principles incorporated in the commandments to results or expectations that will be realized.

Sealing of Family Units

After receiving the endowment, family members can be sealed to each other by those in authority. This ordinance also constitutes a covenant. Promises are made between members of the family and God that, if kept, will qualify the members to participate together in family units through the eternities. Couples are sealed in the temple by those with authority and started on the path that can lead to an eternal family unit. Family relationships will persist beyond death if the conditions of the covenant are met. If children have already been born to a couple who are qualified to be sealed in the temple, these children are also sealed in the family relationship. The children participate in the ordinance as the entire family unit is given the opportunity and promise.

Vicarious Ordinances

All of the covenants described above may be performed vicariously for those who have passed away. These vicarious ordinances are performed in the temple. Each person of record is represented by a proxy as a baptism, confirmation, priesthood ordination (if male), endowment, and sealing covenant is performed. If the individual accepted the principles of the gospel as a result of learning experiences in the spirit world, the ordinances will have validity and will make it possible for each to continue in personal progress. The ordinances imposes nothing upon them, but since these ordinances are required by the Lord and must be performed in mortality, the covenants are made vicariously, and the opportunity is provided for those who have gone ahead. Thus this vicarious work is a great labor of loving service, which blesses not only the potential participant but also the one who gives service.

Additional Ordinances

There are other important ordinances performed under the authority of the priesthood to bless and inspire members of the Church. These ordinances include the following.

Blessing and Naming of Babies

Each new infant is given a name and a father's blessing during the first weeks of life in mortality. The father, or a representative having the authority, officially names the baby and provides it with a father's blessing. Personal inspiration provides the basis of the blessing, but the entire ordinance is performed by the Melchizedek Priesthood authority held by the father and accomplished in the name of Jesus Christ.

Patriarchal Blessings

Certain priesthood holders are ordained patriarchs. The patriarch provides a special recorded blessing for members of the Church when they are sufficiently pre-pared to accept the counsel and opportunity provided through the blessing. The patriarch, acting under the authority given him and through the revelatory influence of the Holy Spirit, proclaims the person's lineage and sets forth those special blessings and instructions for the individual that will serve as a guide in mortality. The blessings are promised on the condition that the individual lives in harmony with admonitions set forth by the patriarch and with the principles of the gospel.

Fathers' Blessings or Priesthood Blessings

A father who is a worthy patriarch in his home and who holds the Melchizedek Priesthood can provide special blessings for his wife and his children. These blessings are typically given when a member of the family is undertaking a new, important phase of life, or when he or she is meeting a special new challenge. It is typical for fathers to give their children blessings when they leave to attend school or are being married. If there is no father in the home able to provide this blessing, a priesthood leader in the Church can perform the service.

Setting Apart

When a member of the Church is given a new calling that requires special authority or inspiration, he or she will be "set apart" for that assignment by someone with priesthood authority. This special blessing at the beginning of a new responsibility provides direction, encouragement, and authority to perform the tasks required.

Blessing of the Sick

Priesthood holders are frequently called upon to provide special blessings for those who are ill. Melchizedek Priesthood holders will participate in pairs to provide this service. One of those involved will anoint the head of the person who is ill with oil that has been consecrated for the healing of the sick through faith. The other will then join with the first and both will lay their hands upon the head of the individual who is sick. One of them gives the person who is ill a special blessing. It is a blessing given through the power of faith under the hands of those with authority. Sometimes the result is an extraordinary healing of the individual who is ill. In all cases the greater perspective of the Lord must be recognized. Everything that can be done to use the knowledge and wisdom available to us at this time should be used. In addition, by extending our faith and the power that is available in the greater truth still beyond our understanding, God is called upon to bless the individual. With His perfect understanding of true principles He can and often does intercede to provide the additional help that is appropriate and consistent with His purposes.

Index